The Lone Shilling

Highland Memories

Albert Philips

BEST WISHES 2018

Albert

First published in 2014 by
For The Right Reasons
(Charity no. SC037781)
Printers & Publishers
60 Grant Street, Inverness

British Library Cataloguing in Publication Data.
A catalogue record of this book is available
from the British Library.

ISBN: 978-1-910205-28-0

DEDICATION

This book is dedicated to my wife Frances Philips, and to all those who fought and offered their services and lives in the First and Second World Wars so we could have our Freedom. Also to my brother Walter Philips (Watty) who died so suddenly on 16th January 2005 and was buried on 22nd January 2005 at Kilvean Cemetery, Inverness. A special mention of thanks to Reverend Fergus Robertson and Mr John Fraser for their kindness and the professional way in which they conducted the ceremony. Sadly, Rena Goodbrand passed away in October 2005 and will be sadly missed.

Cartoon of my brother Watty 1980, by his friend Len Jackson

The photo on the front cover shows the Glen Albyn Distillery as it was in 1979. The vessel on the left is the G.L. (Gate Lifter), moored in the Muirtown Basin. This was used to remove and install the lock-gates on the Caledonian Canal from this view from the west bank of the Canal at Muirtown today can be seen the Muirtown Quay Side with the roof of the Band Q behind. The G.L. was scrapped in the 1980s. The secret pipe mentioned in the distillery stories ran from the Still House seen to the far left in this photograph, underground along the front of the distillery to the building which stands on Telford Street, now used as flats, which was previously the Muirtown Hotel.

ISBN
978-1-905787-39-5

CONTENTS

ACKNOWLEDGEMENT

I would like to give thanks to all the people who have given me support as I have tried to put some of my memories to paper.

First of all, my mother Ann Philips for her help and advice as I have gone through the story of my recent ancestors.

Also to my aunt Rena Goodbrand and to my uncle Johnny Goodbrand, for the use of their amazing memories.

I would also like to thank Stan Williamson and British Waterways, my Aunt Esther Anderson and Donald Fraser's mother Mary Fraser who now stays at Glengarry Road for the use of their photographs which were taken when photography was little known in the highlands.

Also I would like to thank Albert Bird for the use of his Private Diary, and Nancy Watt for the use of her rare photos of canal divers.

Special thanks to Mairi MacArthur for her help and advice, also 'For The Right Reasons' Charity.

A photo which I took about 1979 of the Glen-Albyn Distillery before its demolition . The view will now show the rear view of B & Q Superstore.

FOREWORD

I was born at no. 2 Clachnaharry Road, Inverness on 10th March 1949. My
mother tells me that I am known as a True Clacher, that is a person who was
born in the village of Clachnaharry. At that time children were born in the home
or in a Nursing Home. My brother Len Philips and my cousin Beryl Anderson
are also True Clachers. My brothers are at present still resident in the Inverness
area and my mother lives beside the Caledonian Canal at Canal Terrace on the
same site as the Prefabs in which we lived in the 1960s.
I have gathered the information for this book from members of my family and
friends. My brothers are:
Len Philips
Watty Philips
Sandy Philips
Robert Philips
There was another brother Martin Philips who sadly died at an early age.
If this book does not go into print I hope it will be retained as a family archive.

ALBERT PHILIPS
Sadly as I write this book my brother Watty Philips and Arthur Greig have passed
away and show me how fleeting life can be.

THE CANADIAN BOAT SONG
From the Lone Sheiling of the Misty Island
Mountains divide us and a waste of Seas
Yet still the blood is strong, the heart is Highland
As we in dreams behold the Hebridies.

This is part of the poem 'The Canadian Boat Song', thought to have been written
in 1829. The words are haunting and beautiful and were written by an exiled Scot
thinking of his homeland as he tried to make a life in Canada. This may seem to
be a strange way of starting a book about my family and the Inverness area but
my ancestors came from Broadford on Skye (The Misty Island). Their name was
Robertson. Also this was one of the favourite poems of my old friend William
Vass Wood (Woody), now deceased, and he would often quote them.
A sheiling was a hut or a temporary building where the drover or the shepherd
would take the cattle in the summer months to feed on the rich pastures higher up
the hill.
The women and girls would join them and milk the cows and make butter and
cheese for use in the winter months. This would be a relaxing time and probably
many a romance blossomed at the lone sheiling

My Granny, Ann Gibson on the right and my Great Granny, Isabella Gibson on the left. Outside thedemolished canal bank cottage. Note the railway signal box in the background

A studio portrait of my Great Grandfather

9

MY GREAT-GRANDFATHER

My great-grandfather, the father of Albert Gibson, was Peter Gibson who was a Wool-sorter.   A wool-sorter was an early example of someone involved in recycling rags, similar to a rag and bone man without the bones; a man who went round the streets collecting rags and bones on a horse drawn cart and recycled them, as seen on TV in the program Steptoe and Son.

My great-grandfather owned property on Rose Street in Inverness around 1900. This was warehousing and was part of the Rose Street Foundry. Some of these buildings still survive and are now used as pubs.   He moved to Canal Bank Cottage, Clachnaharry, which is now demolished, but used to stand on an area used as a drying green not far from the railway line, on the canal bank leading to the Sea-Lock house.

I have two photographs taken about the time of the First World War.   One Photo was taken outside the cottage.   The woman seated is my great-grandmother Isabella Kennedy and the woman standing is my grandmother Ann Mackinnon Mackay who married Albert Gibson.   Note the railway signal box in the background as it stands today.

The other is a studio photo and shows my great-grandfather Peter Gibson standing behind my grandfather Albert Gibson who is in uniform ready to go to the front in the First World War.   He was fifteen years old.   The two women are my grand-father's sister Barbara Gibson and Nell Thomson a local villager.   My grandfather went to the front and was spotted by an officer who sent him home until he was seventeen years old. He returned when he was seventeen and fought in the First World War.

My grandfather Albert Gibson and his brothers Magnus Gibson and Robert Gibson all fought in the war.   Sadly Robert did not return; he was killed at the battle of The Marne in France and is buried at Lillers Communal Cemetery, Pas De Calais. He was 29 years old and died on Tuesday 28th September 1915.
When the three brothers set off from Clachnaharry village to join the regiment of the Cameron Highlanders, my grandfather told my mother that Robert kept looking back at the village and my grandfather thought Robert knew he would not see it again.   I think it is important to remember those who fought and died so we could have freedom and do so in this Book.

Albert Gibson and Magnus Gibson and my grandmother's brother George Mackay are all mentioned in the book *The Sword Of The North* by Dugald

Macechern whose father was Parish Minister for Inverness at the time of the First World War. My mother knew the Macechern family and would often talk of them. I have the good fortune of owning a copy of this book. It has some 670 pages and 630 photo engravings. It includes all the Regiments that fought in the First World War from the North of Scotland and some Regiments from the East and West of Scotland. I search this book for relations and friends if asked. It probably contains thousands of names and records and records the Battles and Honours of the Regiments. As you will gather this book does not leave my sight. Do not disregard my book now as being morbid and uninteresting as the more lighthearted stories are in the second half. I have read a lot and I know the author has to capture the interest of the reader early on. But my family and their involvement in the First World War are important to me and I would like to record it.

This is a poem I have written in memory of those who fought and died so that we could have our freedom.

THE OLD ONES

Don't forget the old ones as we sing and laugh and dance

Those who fought for our freedom, in those far off fields of France

They say that they had fallen so many years ago

But the truth is far more haunting. What a terrible way to go,

To live in mud and trenches as the War went on and on

And suffer fear and hardship so we may grow and live on

'Over the top' and 'forward', the cry would go up

As fear would grip their insides; As they thought their numbers up.

Who knows how our generation would face such an awful task

But as it is we will never know and the old ones we cannot ask

ALEXANDER MACKAY

Before I leave this period I would like to mention my grandmother's father Alexander Mackay who worked as a Pattern Maker at the Rose Street Foundry. He was the Gaelic Presenter for the St Mary's Gaelic Church on Church Street and was the Superintendent of the Sunday Schools for the Parish of Inverness, and lived at no 114 Church Street which is now demolished. The church is now used as a Bookshop and is owned by Mr Leakey.

This is a studio photograph of my Grandmother, Ann Mackinnon Mackay in her overalls and cap when she worked as a welder for the Thornbush Slipway. This photograph was taken during the First World War, 1914-1918

This is a photograph taken by my Aunt Ester Anderson about 1953 with the old suspension bridge over the River Ness in the background along with Inverness Castle and Castle Tolmie. The wall in the photograph is now demolished. This shot was taken on what is now the pavement opposite the British Legion Club on Huntly Street.

The woman with the pram (and what a pram it is) is my Grandmother, Ann Gibson, with my brother Watty and my cousin Beryl.

AN EARLY AIRCRAFT PASSENGER

Before Dalcross was the airport for Inverness the Inverness Aerodrome was in the Longman in Inverness. In about 1934 the Inverness Courier ran a competition and the prize was a flight in an airplane piloted by Captain Fresson the pioneer of air flight in the Highlands. My granny, Ann Gibson, won the prize and flew round Inverness from the Longman Aerodrome. My mother, then a child, watched as my granny boarded the plane and was terrified until it landed again.

A picture painted in 1984 showing a scene in the Longman with Captain Fresson at the start of the first Airmail Service in Great Britain is on display at Dalcross Airport.

MY GRANDPARENTS AND FAMILY

At the time of The Second World War my granny had given birth to six daughters Margaret, Mary, Ann and Isobel (the twins), Esther and Rina, short for Alexanderina. My grandfather worked for the aluminium factory at Foyers on the south side of Loch Ness. The aluminium factory was bombed during the war. It was a prime target as aluminium was used in the manufacture of planes. It was not a direct hit; the bomb landed in sand which took the blast but a wall of the factory was damaged and one man lost a leg in the bombing. At the local school the children were playing in the playground at the time of the bombing and waved at the pilots and the pilots waved back. Of course the pilots could have opened fire on the children but did not.

After the Second World War the Gibson family moved to Inverness and my grandfather got a job as a lockkeeper for the Caledonian Canal. He asked the manager if he would be allowed to fight in the war but the manager would not allow it. My mother told me the hours of work were from dawn to dusk which must have been a very long day especially in the summer.

At this time the lock gates were opened and closed manually. You may have seen the capstans used to do this now used as this garden ornaments or set beside the canal. There would be long wooden poles inserted into the capstan and four or six men would walk round opening or closing the gates. There was a metal pole below the capstan and a chain would wrap round a cog and move the lock gate. Before this could be done the water level had to be altered by opening or closing the sluice gates at the bottom of the lock gate. A tee-key was inserted at the top of the lock gate and turned clockwise or anticlockwise to move the sluice gate at the bottom of the gate. Of course this is now done automatically by pressing buttons or by moving a lever.

POACHING

My Aunty Rena told me as a child she went with my grandfather to set his net. At that time they lived at the Sea-Lock House. He would set his net in September or October to catch the Kessock Herring which would swim in shoals round the Beauly Firth. The Kessock Herring were well known when I was a boy and the Navigation Lights of the trawlers would be seen at night fishing for these herring. Today I see no boats fishing in the Beauly Firth and the Kessock Herring have probably been wiped out by over fishing and pollution.

He would set his net at low tide on the beach at the back of the back bank of the Canal and would return at high tide to see if he had caught anything. Rena went with him and when the net was pulled in there was a salmon in it. My Grandfather asked
Rena to run back to the house and get a cloth or a tea towel to wrap the fish in, which she did. He wrapped the fish in the tea towel and took it to a hotel where it was sold. These things were done to supplement the meager wages and to put food on the table.

I can also remember as a boy going with George Ralph who was a Lock Keeper in his rowing boat to net salmon and sea trout at the mouth or entrance to the Caledonian Canal. He would row or scull his boat in a circle and in a very short time he would have salmon and sea trout in the boat. He would then cycle through the village of Clachnaharry and sell the fish to the locals and take the rest to Inverness to sell to the fishmongers.

Until recent times salmon and sea trout would run through the canal as they would run through the River Ness. The salmon par must have found their way from the tributaries of Loch Ness and instead of returning to the sea by the River Ness came through the Caledonian Canal. This must have been a long and time-consuming journey as they would have to wait for a boat to go through the locks before they could continue. Salmon par grow into smolts and eventually head to sea to grow into salmon, returning by smell or instinct to the place of their birth and continue their journey through the Caledonian Canal. As a boy I can remember seeing large amounts of salmon and sea trout in the Sea-Lock Basin at Clachnaharry. We could not catch them with rod and line although I know some were removed using other methods. (Sculling is rowing a boat using only one oar inserted into a slot at the back of the boat.)

CANAL DIVERS

Maintenance of the Canal up to the nineteen sixties was carried out by the Canal workforce. I can remember in the late nineteen fifties watching the Canal Diver working in the locks at Clachnaharry. I could see the bubbles on the surface and the tubes and ropes going underwater. The air was pumped down to him by a manual pump which was operated from a metal punt on the surface. This was called the Diving Coble.

I remember when he came up after working underwater for some time. They used a rope and signaled by pulls on the rope. The diver would give so many pulls on the rope to signal he wanted to come up.

When they got him onto the coble his brass helmet was removed and he asked for the empty Stratton milk bottle which he passed inside the suit to relieve himself. The man on the pump was called The Dummy because he was deaf and dumb.

The Health and Safety Act was unknown at this time and the diver was one of the canal lock-keepers or anyone suitable to be a diver.
My grandfather had a bad experience when diving in the canal. His fellow workers nearly killed him. The hand pump on the coble was normally operated by The Dummy who was deaf and dumb and would not be distracted by sound or blethering and would concentrate on turning the hand pump so the right amount of air was pumped underwater to the diver. On this day the Dummy was not on the pump and the person was turning the handle too quickly and pumping too much air into the diving suit. The result was the diver started to lift off the bottom of the canal and float to the surface. When someone saw what was happening my grandfather was pulled onto the diving coble and was in a semi-conscious state. A doctor was called and he was in bed for several days recovering. After this he refused to dive again.

THE LIVE SHELL

During the Second World War ships would dock at the Muirtown Basin and be loaded with shells and then go to Scapa Flow. The shells were taken by rail to the quayside at Muirtown on the spur railway-line which came off the main railway-line. This line ran along the back bank of the canal and the remains of this line may still be seen. The shells would be off-loaded from the trucks and transferred onto the ships at the quayside. As the shells were being transferred one of the shells slipped through the sling and went over the side and sank to the bottom of the canal. My grandfather, Albert Gibson, who worked as a Lock keeper or a diver was asked to go down and retrieve the shell. This he did and the shell was recovered.

Today we find it difficult to understand that this could happen, as today this would be a job for the Army Bomb Disposal Unit. But it did happen and the story was told to me by my aunt Rena who was a young girl at the time. Of course, if anything had gone wrong and the shell had exploded it would have blown up a large part of Inverness.

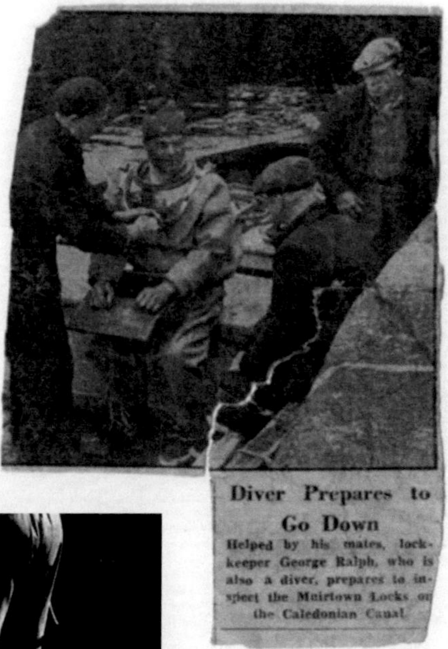

Diver Prepares to Go Down

Helped by his mates, lock-keeper George Ralph, who is also a diver, prepares to inspect the Muirtown Locks on the Caledonian Canal.

A newspaper clipping showing George Ralph being prepared for diving

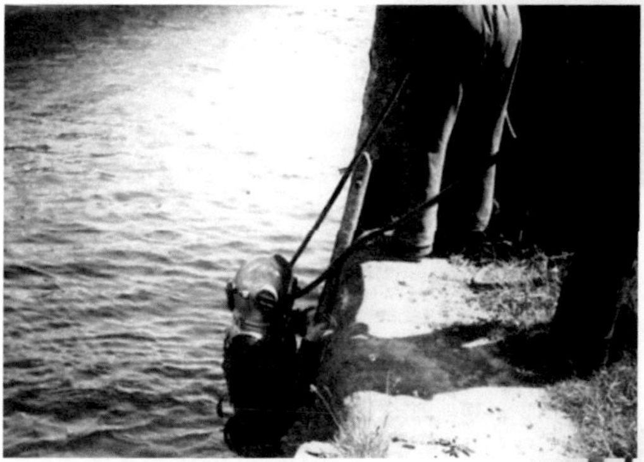

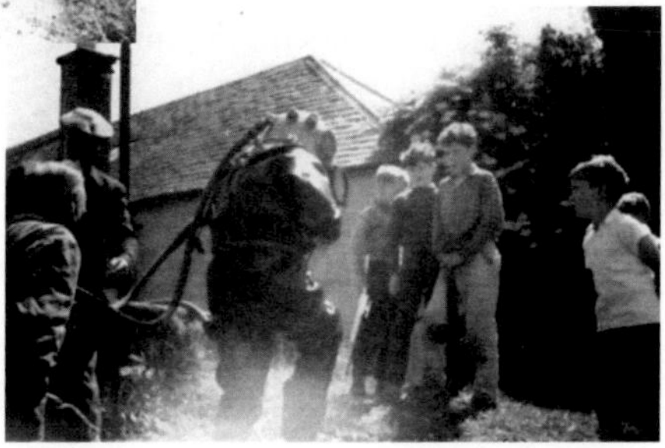

Photos showing a canal diver emerging from the canal at Clachnaharry Locks

This is a photograph taken in the late 1950's of my grandfather, Albert Gibson with a fine catch of Brown Trout caught on Loch Mullardoch, above the village of Cannich, north of Beauly.

MY GRANDFATHER

There must be about fifty trout, up to a pound in weight in the photo. He would have been the guest of his nephew, Jock Gibson and his wife Rita Gibson. The reason there were large catches of fish at this time was because of the abundance of feeding for the trout available after the recent flooding of the area to form the Hydro-Electric Dam. The feeding would have come from the worms, slugs and insects which were in the banks of the glen prior to the flooding. The trout would have put on a lot of weight in a very short time because of the rich feeding. Rita and Jock lived at Jock's Lodge which stands on the left hand side of the road before you enter the village of Cannich.

Although this photograph shows my grandfather with a spinning rod, and what looks like a Mitchell 300 spinning reel, he was a keen fly-fisher and I would watch him as a boy, as he sat at his fly-fishing vice, tying up his favourite patterns of fly- such as The Bloody Butcher, The Mallard and Claret and the Black Pennel. He would look in the sewing box for pieces of coloured wool and use the feathers from a starling for the wings. I dare say he used the feathers from his budgies, as he was a keen budgie breeder and had an aviary in the shed at the rear of Elgol, in Clachnaharry Road.

I remember as a boy being shouted at by my grandfather when he came home from his job as a lock-keeper. To the front of his shed, there was a metal cover at

18

the entrance, which was over a channel which ran along the front of the shed. He had his foot over one end of the channel and a spade over the other end. The metal cover would have been about three feet long. My grandfather had seen a rat go under the metal cover and had trapped it underneath. He told me to go into the shed and get the graip. When he lifted the spade to let the rat escape, I was to kill the rat as it tried to escape. As the rat made its bid for freedom, I made a stab at it but it escaped. Of course, at about nine years of age, I was a little young to be spearing rats with a garden fork and my grandfather came out with some words I did not understand before I was dismissed. From then on, I have had a dislike for these creatures and I suppose this is quite reasonable.

I can also remember my grandfather and my father making a Green Heart salmon fishing rod in the kitchen of Elgol House. They planed down the blank square pieces of the wood used to make the rod and finished off the rod section by smoothing it down to the correct diameter with a piece of glass. After this they fitted the reel fittings and then fitted the metal ferrules which joined the pieces together. They finished the rod of by whipping on the eyes and varnishing the rod.

This may seem like a lot of work but money was scarce and this would have saved a lot of money compared to a shop bought fishing rod. No doubt my father would have put this rod to good use as he would continue using the skills taught to him by his father, this is ripping salmon from a river pool on the great salmon rivers of Scotland. My father's family came from Dufftown and he was probably taught the skills which put him in jail for poaching salmon on what is one of the most famous salmon rivers, the River Spey.

When I was employed as a welder at the Oil Fabrication Yard in Ardersier in the 1970's, I spoke to a crane driver who told me he had worked with my father on the Hydro-Electric Schemes in the Highlands. I had not known my father as a child as he left my mother in the 1950's, with five boys to bring up. He told me that my father was a desperate character and no salmon trapped in the rivers, when the Hydro-Electric Dams were being constructed, were safe and he would remove them, no doubt by ripping them out of the water. I will not go into details of this cruel practice but I will say that it involved the use of treble hooks attached to a heavy duty nylon cast which was dragged through the salmon pool. He also told me the stink from the workshop at the Hydro-Electric Scheme was awful, as my father attempted to make whisky with a spirit still.

I may add that I continue the family interest in fishing although in a more legal fashion and tie my own fishing flies. I enjoy a days trout fishing during my annual holidays

In this British Waterways photograph taken at the time of the mechanisation of the lock-gates, the small figure of my brother Watty Philips, with his fishing rod, can be seen to the left of the circle painted on the Railway Swing Bridge at Clachnaharry. He would have been about eight years old. The photograph is taken from inside the Control Room at Clachnaharry.

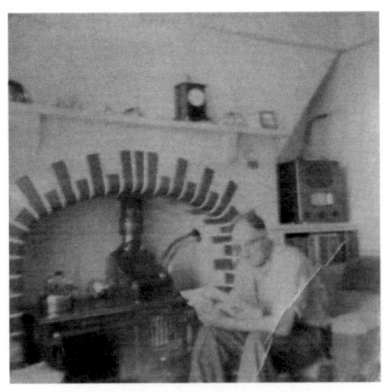

This photograph was taken inside Elgol on Clachnaharry Road in the late 1950s. It shows my grandfather in front of the cast iron range. This had an oven and hot plates to boil a kettle or a pan. The pipe on the right hand side would carry hot water to a tank. Note the wireless(radio) on the RHS, the latest technology of that time, a valve radio used to listen to the Scottish Home Service. etc.

THE LOCH NESS MONSTER

In August 1950 my aunt Margaret Cargill, her mother-in-law Marion Cargill, my aunt Rena Macgilivary and my cousins Alick Cargill and James Macgilivary were in an Austin Seven car driven by my uncle Jimmy Macgilivary. This may seem a lot of people to be in a car but my cousins Alick and James were children.

Rena saw the Monster in the middle of the loch and shouted to stop the car. It was about seven o'clock in the evening and the loch was flat calm. They got out of the car. There were no other cars on the road and they watched the Monster as it swam along the middle of the loch. The place where they stopped was looking down on Urquhart Castle. They watched it for ten minutes as it swam along the middle of the loch before it dived.

There was a double-decker bus driving along the Dores Road on the other side of the loch and Rena estimated the size of the monster to be about thirty feet long. She said it was a dark colour similar to the colour of an elephant and she could see a long neck and two humps and the wake it left as the tail end of the creature propelled it along. At the same part of the road but walking in the opposite direction were a couple who Jimmy Macgilivary knew but as they were walking in the opposite direction they saw nothing even though, as is often the case in monster sightings they had binoculars and a camera.

Believe it or believe it not that is the story as told to me by my aunt Rena Macgilivary, now Rena Goodbrand.

GL at Clachnaharry slipway. Date unknown.

The Scott II in its former glory on Loch Ness, date unknown. I believe the Scott II is now under restoration.

Wooden Sealock Jetty: Clachnaharry under construction.
Note the diving coble and diver. Date unknown, early 20ᵗʰ Century.

Lock-Gate on Slipway, Clachnaharry

Photo taken about 1960. Note the gate on the RHS across the road.
These were replaced by lift-up barriers.

MY FATHER

My Father, Walter Macdonald Philips, came from Dufftown. He fought in the Second World War and was in The Gordon Highlanders. He was captured at St Valery and when he was being transported to a prison of war camp he slipped off the back of a lorry, rolled into a ditch and waited until it was safe to move off into the woods.

He lived in the woods for two weeks on wild berries. He must have been hungry. He went into a village in Brittany and was looking in the window of a baker's shop when a woman approached him and asked him if he was English. My Father said he was Scottish. She took him to their home, which was a Chateau in Brittany, and he worked on a farm. She was Madam Charpion and she lived with her husband Count Charpion at the Chateau. They dyed his hair brown as he had red hair and nobody who lived locally had red hair.

During the day he worked on the farm owned by the Charpion family and at night they hid him in the oast house. They called him To-To which is the same as the dog in the film *Wizard of Oz*. The dog's name was used as an alarm call to let my Father know if the German troops were coming. In the evening the Germans would come on their motorbikes to get food from the farm. My Father would hear the sound of the motorbike approaching and he would be terrified until he heard them leaving.

Eventually arrangements were made for my Father to be taken over the Pyrenees Mountains to France and on to Marseilles.

Guides were paid to do this but this was a very dangerous thing to do as the guides would sometimes take the money and when they got into the mountains they would shoot the prisoners and leave the bodies in the mountains.

My Father made it to the Marseilles and found a boat sailing to Britain. During this period he was suffering from a grumbling appendix which burst. He was treated in a hospital in France before he could make his way home. He sailed from France to Aberdeen and was treated in hospital before he finally made it home.

My Mother told me that after the war ended my Father would be terrified at the sound of a motorbike engine. Of course at that time there was no post trauma counseling for those who survived the war, they just had to get on with it.

MY FATHER THE POACHER

My Father would go poaching salmon in 1951. My Mother said his Father taught him how to RIP Salmon (sniggle salmon).

I can remember as a boy of about five years old seeing the bath at our home number 21 Hawthorn Drive, Inverness, half full of salmon. My mother said the fish were thirty and forty pounders. He would sell the fish to local hotels until the police arrived and took him away. My Father ended up in prison for poaching and he was the first person in Scotland to be prosecuted under the 1951 Fresh Water Act to protect salmon and sea trout. He argued that nobody had the right to own these fish as they were not put in the river or sea by those who brought out the protection order, but he was found guilty and was sent down for forty days.

At this time Madam and Count Charpion, the people who had helped him escape after the battle of St Valery, visited my Mother in Inverness. They tried to help my Father and pleaded for his release from prison but were unsuccessful. He served his sentence.

Walter Philips of Inverness with Mme Germaine Charpion.

JIMMY MACGILLIVRAY

My Uncle Jimmy MacGillivray lived at 18, Duncraig Street, Inverness at the time of the Second World War. He can be seen in the picture of the casualty list printed by *The People's Journal* dated July 27th 1940. He is the third from the left in the second row. He was captured at St Valery. The prisoners were marched through France to the Prisoner of War Camps and on the way through French people would try and give food to the prisoners, but they had nothing to hold the food in. Jimmy came out of the line of prisoners and went into the basement of a street side café to try and get something to hold the food, as all he had was a small mess-tin. He tried to get a container from the staff in the café. As he turned round to return to the line of prisoners a member of the S.S. was holding a revolver to his head. Jimmy thought his number was up but he showed the German his mess-tin and the German did not shoot.

The photos taken inside the Prisoner of War Camp show the prisoners in good shape. This was because they were given an extra plate of soup each day as the Germans needed them to work in the coalmines in Poland. Jimmy was fit and survived the war, but it probably affected his health, as he died quite young soon after the war. The photos of the British prisoners taken inside the camp fascinate me. My auntie Rena (Jimmy's wife after the War) told me this was because the British Red Cross insisted that two letters or photos had to be sent home to relatives twice a year. The backs of the photos have the censored stamp showing Stalag XX1A and Jimmy's prison number 303. Any writing by the prisoners on the back of the photos was in pencil. If the censor did not like what was written he could rub it out; pen writing was not allowed. One photo shows the football team and one photo shows what looks like a party, probably Christmas.

Before the war Jimmy played for the Inverness Thistle Football Club and after the war he played for the Caledonian Football Club. In about 1954 Jimmy played for Caley in a qualifying cup final against Morton, which was held in Ibrox in Glasgow, home of the famous Rangers. Rena has the medal awarded to Jimmy and she said she was shown the premises and the trophy room of this famous club.

His son James MacGillivray, who is still living in Inverness, survives Jimmy. Rena has re-married and is now Rena Goodbrand. She is married to Johnny Goodbrand who worked man and boy for B.T. laying cables and equipment in all parts of Scotland. Johnny is now retired and Rena and Johnny live in Scorguie in Inverness.

Photographs of the British prisoners taken inside the prisoner of war camp

Photographs taken by Germans inside Stalag 11A during the Second World War, showing Jimmy and his fellow prisoners.

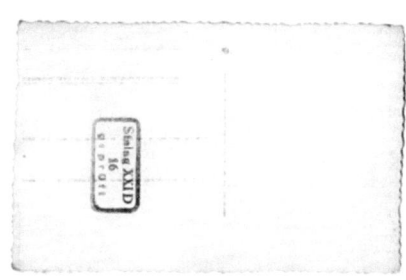

The backs of the photographs have the censored stamp showing Stalag XX1A and Jimmy's prison number 303

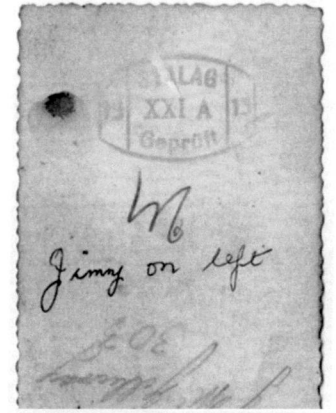

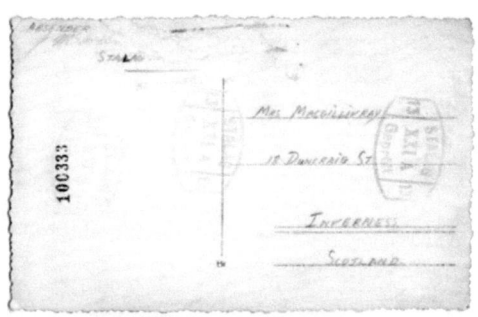

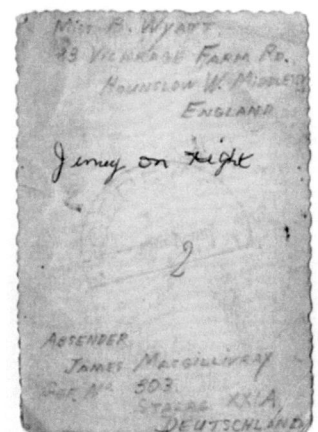

Pte. Michael Hassen, 21 Smith Avenue, Inverness (missing); right—Pte. Jas. W. A. R. Fraser, 28 Argyle Street, Inverness (missing).

L.-Cpl. A. Cameron, 15 Dochfour Drive, Inverness (missing); L.-Cpl. Hamish Barclay, 64 Dunain Road, Inverness (missing).

Pte. Harry M'Donald, 25 Glencruitten Drive, Oban, A. and S.H. (missing); right, Seaman Murdo Alick Lamont, Kilmuir, Skye (missing).

Pte. James M'Gillivray, 18 Duncraig Street, Inverness (missing); Pte. James A. Macrae, Cradlehall Farm, Inverness (missing).

Pte. Wm. M'Kenzie Inverness (missing M'Donald, Dalhallo (mi

L.-Cpl. George MacBain and L.-Cpl. M' in, son of Mrs MacBain, Caledonian House, Kingussie (missing).

L.-Cpl. Jack M'Donald, 38 King Street, Inverness (missing); Pte. Alex. Robertson, 115 West Drive, Inverness (missing).

Pte. James Mackay ness (missing); Viewfield, Cu

Cpl. A. M. Wiseman, 32 Friars Street, Inverness (missing); Pte. Tom Smith, 36

Sgt. Alistair Mackenzie and Sgt. Gordon Mackenzie, 21 Innes Street, Inverness,

C.S.M. James Sava Inverness

30

Pte. D. W. M'Gillivray, 63 Dochfour Drive, Inverness (missing); Pte. Eric Dickson, 7 Dunain Road, Inverness (missing).

Pte. Roderick Grant, 71 Castle Street, Inverness (missing); C.S.M. Fox, 418 Lochalsh Road, Inverness (missing).

Jallfeary Road, Pte. James Cottage, Culcabock sing).

Pte. Allan Grant, Kerrow Cottage, Kingussie (missing); C.S.M. Cecil Mac-Kintosh, M.C. Camerons, Birchfield, Kingussie, prisoner of war.

Piper Peter M'Rae and Pte. Wm. M'Rae, twin sons of Mrs M'Rae, Mavsebill Lodge, Nairn (missing). Wm. resides Bungalow, Strathpeffer.

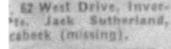

62 West Drive, Inver- Pte. Jack Sutherland, cabock (missing).

Cpl. D.ff. Thornbush Road, Inverness (missing); Pte. A. Macdonald, 80 West Drive, Inverness (missing).

Pte. Allan Macrae, 43 Friars Street, Inverness (missing); Pte. Geo. MacLennan, 15 Friars Street (missing).

e, 29 Abban Street, Frederick Shand

Pte. W. Mackay, 49 King Street, Inverness (missing); Cpl. Opair Munro, well-

Pte. Kenneth MacLennan, 57 Lochalsh Road, Inverness (missing)

31

Sergt. H. Morrison, Tomich, Invergordon, Seaforths (missing); Pte. D. R. Bell, Saltburn, Invergordon (missing).

Sergt. Charles Mackenzie, Sergt. John Mackenzie, L.-Cpl. A. J. Mackenzie, sons of Mr and Mrs Mackenzie, 25 Harrowden Road, Inverness, (m issing).

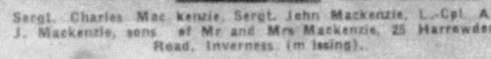

Pte. P. Bernardi, died in a military hospital, and Pte. Scotti Bernardi, missing—sons of Mrs Bernardi, Bridge Street, Inverness.

Pte. John Duff, Invergordon Mains (missing); Pte. J. Rhind, Fairlea, Saltburn (missing).

Pte. Lionel Ian Mack Dingwall (missing); son of Mr and M Cottage, Deil

. Urquhart, Brightmony, Auldearn (missing); Pte. John Grant, Chattan Gardens, Nairn (missing).

Pte. Duncan MacLeod, No. 6 Melbost Stornoway (missing); Pte. Reddy Fergusen, Bernera, Lewis (missing).

Trooper William R Tain (missing); Cpl. forth, Tain

C. Urquhart, Elliot Road, Inverden (missing); Pte. Dryden Ross, tage, Saltburn, Invergordon (missing).

Gunner J. B. Stewart, 8 Soroba Park Terrace, Oban, Anti-Tank Battery (missing); right, Ian Brown, Lorn Terrace, Oban, Anti-Tank Battery (missing).

Gunner Roderick cruitten Drive, Oba (missing); Gunner Miller Road,

32

Pte. David Mac-
Donald, Hillhead,
Dalcross (missing).

Pte. Ian Mackenzie, Kerrowaird, Dalcross
(missing); Pte. J. Davidson, A.M.P.C.,
110 Lochaish Road, Inverness (missing).

Pte. Donald Campbell, son of Mr and Mrs
J. Campbell, Navity, Cromarty (missing);
and Piper John M'Iver, their son-in-law
(missing).

..enzie, 26 Hill Street,
Pte. Henry Lindie,
Mrs Lindie, Pitnicol
..ny (missing).

Pte. Wm. C. Macleod, son of Rev. D.
Macleod, Saltburn (missing); Pte. A.
M'Donald, 5 Inglis Road, Invergordon
(missing).

Pte. John Macdonald and (right) Pte.
Hugh Macdonald, sons of Mr and Mrs
Macdonald, Hartfield Street, Tain
(missing).

..ess, Lo..Lieuts.
George..hland, Sea-
.. (miss...).

Sergt. H. Stewart, son of Mrs Stewart,
Alness (wounded); Pte. Wm. Macleod,
Balintraid (missing).

Pte. John Cross, Murray Road, Invergordon (missing); Pte. R. Speed, Saltburn, Invergordon (missing).

Mac..enzie, 11 Glen-
.., Anti-Tank Battery
Arch. MacFarlane, 11
Oban (missing).

Gunner ..., MacInnes, 3 Lochavullin
Terrace, Oban (missing); right, Gunner
Arch. MacInnes, Aird's Close, Oban
(missing).

Sergt. Allan M'Kenzie, Argylls, Balla-
chulish (prisoner of war); Sergt. James
MacDougall, Gordons, Kinlochleven
(missing).

33

THE ROSE

It is difficult to think that a beautiful Moss Rose could cause the loss of a thumb joint but it did.

My aunty Isobel, my mother's twin sister – who, I may add, put many a good dinner in front of us when we had little money - was gardening. Pruning and picking roses at May Cottage at the top of Canal Road where my granny lived at the time of the Second World War. A thorn from the rose bush went into her thumb and festered and poisoned the joint. At this pre-Second World War period penicillin was unknown and my mother told me the only painkiller was a bible which Isobel held onto as she tried to sleep at night but could not because of the pain. My mother said the doctor lanced the wound and a tinkle could be heard as the top joint of the thumb fell into a small surgical tray. Her thumb may have been cauterised as it looked like a round blob.

My mother has one of the same moss rose bushes in her garden at Canal Terrace in Inverness and I was successful in taking cuttings from it. I have two bushes growing in my garden at Scorguie in Inverness. It is a very old rose with a beautiful scent and could go back to Victorian times. It is pink in colour.
The school photo shows Isobel as a child and she bears a remarkable resemblance to my daughter Helen and my niece Emma Philips.

Isobel

THE LONE SHILLING

When we lived at 21 Hawthorn Drive about 1954, I attended Dalneigh primary School.

At this time we were very poor and there was no money in the home. I say home because a house can be a home although there is no money in it. I went to school in the morning and as I left the playground on my way home for lunch, I found a shilling. Of course lunch is a very posh name for this meal as it probably consisted of a piece on jam (a sandwich). If you were lucky.

At this time I was about five years old. My mother had no money to put in the gas meter to cook our food and I gave her the shilling. She took it and said she would not have me branded a thief and told me to take it back to school and see if anyone claimed it. She did this knowing there was no money in our home to put in the gas meter to cook whatever food we had for our supper and the chances of somebody finding out that I had found a shilling was practically impossible.

At the end of the afternoon the teacher said to me that nobody had claimed the shilling and I was given it to take home to my mother. My mother put the shilling in the gas meter and cooked whatever food we had. You may find this hard to believe, but there was no other money in our home.

This shows my mother as being a very Christian person as she would have rather have muddled through with no money to put in the gas meter to cook our food. We were brought up in a Christian home and although we were very poor we would attend Sunday School and the Dalneigh Church. It shows how things have changed. When I visit secondary schools in Inverness and read gas meters in my job I see one and two pence pieces discarded as dross and thrown in the corridors and playground as being worthless when we as children needed every penny and shilling to survive.

I spoke to a Janitor at one of these Schools and he told me they collected these coins as they swept up and donated them to Charity. Just think what my mother could have done with all those coins. I write this story to show the younger generation how hard times were when I was young although I would not wish this life on them.

THE GALA

In the 1950s the village of Clachnaharry held its Annual Gala. The Galas shown in the photographs took place about 1960.

Everyone joined in and the local lorries and vehicles would parade from Clachnaharry down Telford Street and up Academy Street, along High Street and end up back at the Blackpark Hall. The Hall was at the top of Scorguie Road and Blackpark Terrace. This area is now a play park. Everyone would dress up and each lorry would have a different theme including A School Room, The Beatniks, Tropical Island and Man in Space, including Yuri Gagarin, the first man in space. There would be horse drawn carriages and coaches and a horse drawn milk float.

A split screen lorry, driven by (Neeny) Ian MacLeod ready to go into the Gala parade.

Every year in the 1950s the Gala Queen would be crowned at the start of the Gala. She would be chosen from one of the local Clachnaharry school children. She would have two Attendants and a Pageboy. The procession would leave the village led by a pipe band followed by a horse drawn carriage which carried the Gala Queen and her Attendants. Behind her coach were the cars and floats and the procession would make its way to Inverness Town centre.

In the procession there was a converted stage coach on the top of which were children dressed up as soldiers. The stagecoach belonged to Falconers Garage on Tomnahurich Street. A bracket was fitted to the front of the stagecoach so it could be pulled by a lorry. The stagecoach was dismantled and burnt at Clachnaharry after the Gala in 1960 or 1961. It would have been an original stagecoach used by Falconers Garage for excursions before the use of buses and cars. In the 1950s and 60s very few people would own a car.

The photographs shown are rare, as very few people owned a camera.
They would have been taken on a Brownie or a box camera. Below is a photo
showing the Gala Queen being crowned by Provost Wotherspoon's wife.

From left to right: Simon Fraser. Ellen Macdonald. Provost Wotherspoon's wife. Evelyn
Sutherland?   ?Eileen Junor.

The Gala Procession leaving Clachnaharry, the carriage driver is Colin Greig with the
Gala Queen and her attendants. Gala Queen, unknown, her attendants are Moira and
Cathleen Johnston and John Macleod.

From left to right: Len Philips, Robert Jack, Rita Gibson, ?(possibly one of the Murray triplets). Rena MacGillivray, Watty Philips, Ann Philips, Valerie Gibson,?

A photo taken as the procession arrives at the Blackpark Hall.My brother, Watty Philips is dressed up as Yuri Gagaren, the first man in space. The gable of the Blackpark Hall can be seen on the right hand side. This building was demolished in the 1960's

The Beatnik Float leaving the village of Clachnaharry. Note the Landrover owned by Macleods Caravans, the registration PST 16 is still in use today.

Back at the Blackpark Hall. Notice the Split-Screen VW owned by Carl the eel fisher. I can remember watching Carl as he baited his fish traps (fish boxes) and lowered them into the sea-lock on a length of rope. He would pull them up the next day and they would be full of eels. He would put the eels into tanks on the back of his VW and take them away to sell. In the photo is Carl, my aunty Rena and ?

Arriving back at The Blackpark Hall.Mary Fraser. Rena Macgilivary. Isobel Gibson, Netta Urquhaurt.Front: Simon Fraser. Robert Bird. Robert Philips. The field in the background is now the Scorguie Housing Estate and what is now Swanson Avenue.

A Photo taken inside The Blackpark Hall.

This is the stage-coach taking part in a Clachnaharry Gala

My aunt Esther told me that this stage-coach belonged to a company called Falconers whose premises were on Tomnahurich Street in Inverness. This form of transport would have been used in Inverness before the car. The stage-coach was burned at Clachnaharry when Galas no longer took place.

Another split screen lorry used in the Gala Parade. This is probably the Lorry owned by Bengy the Coalman. Note the Pre-Fabs at Blackpark Terrace.
The notice on the radiator is advertising The Children's Concert to be held in The Blackpark Hall on 20th of July 1960.

A Milk Float taking part in the Gala

ROUND AND ABOUT BLACKPARK

In the 1960's there was a Caravan Park opposite the Blackpark Petrol Station. It was used by travelling people and I can remember their lorries full of carpets which they would sell locally and return to the park in the evening. The site was run by Wullie Mason who lived in a corrugated iron roofed house which was beside the Toll House. All that remains of the Park and house is the brick toilet which can be seen beside the road among the trees.

I worked for the McHardy family who owned the petrol station when I was a boy. I worked part-time at the petrol station and in the evening there were very few cars calling in to be filled up with petrol as there were very few cars on the roads in 1960. I think Petrol was about 3 and 8 pence a gallon, in the old money of course. I can remember Colin McHardy asking a gypsy woman who was staying at the caravan park to read his palm. This she did but asked for her palm to be crossed with silver. Colin opened the till and took out a shilling and gave it to the gypsy.

A woman who stayed in one of the big houses opposite the caravan site took exception to the travelling people staying across the road and told a gypsy woman of her dislike of them. The gypsy told her that soon they would be moving on but would come back in the following summer and when they came back they would be staying in the caravan site but the woman would no longer be staying in her house. This proved to be true as there was a problem with the deeds of the house and when the travelling people returned the following year the woman had moved.

THE PREFABS

Prefabricated Houses to most people mean the Aluminium Houses erected after The Second World War to accommodate those returning after the War to find a shortage of housing. These Prefabs were sited in Inverness at Blackpark Terrace and Wyvis Place.

The Aluminium Houses were very up-to-date at the time they were erected and were some of the first houses to have a fitted kitchen including a gas fridge. The shortage of housing after the war meant that some people had nowhere to live and would squat in the wooden Nissan Huts used by the Forces during the War. These huts were at Raigmore, The Bught and in the Longman. The local authorities would sympathize with these people and would put running water into the huts to try and make them more comfortable. I lived in Prefabs at Blackpark Terrace and Canal road in the 1960's before they were demolished.

In a recent television program people were still living in Prefabs in 2003 and were very reluctant to leave them; this is remarkable as the houses were thought to have a life of about ten years. There are prefabricated houses still standing in Inverness in the form of the Swedish wooden houses in Dalneigh. Up until the 1960's the area that is now Blackpark Terrace as far as Firthview Road was covered in Prefabs after that it was fields as far as the Craig Phadrig Forest. On the other side of the road of what is now Firthview Road were sheep pens used by the local farmers to dip and shear their sheep.

I used to feel sorry for the sheep if they were sheared by Donny Mackay on his return from a visit to The Clachnaharry Inn as when the sheep he had sheared were let loose there would be lumps taken out of them as Donny tried his skills when under the influence of alcohol. Donny had a farm on the top road above Clachnaharry. This road is now a path opposite the end of Firthview Road. It continued past Woodside Crescent and came out above Delmore. Sometimes Donny would not be successful in driving his van home to his farm after an evening in the Clachnaharry Inn and would have to make arrangements next day to have it removed from a ditch into which he had driven it.

The only other house above the Prefabs on Blackpark Terrace was Scorguie House whose owners bred Skye Terriers. My brother Watty and myself who were skint went up to the house to see if they needed any odd jobs done. All they had was the job of mucking out the dog kennels. This we did and what a stinking job that was. We earned a couple of shillings each for this but we did not volunteer our services again. Scorguie House still stands and is at the top of what is now Croft Road.

In one of the Prefabs lived a man who was a wood-cutter and worked in Craig Phadrig Forest. We would go with him as he removed the trees he had cut from the forest He would do this by using chains and a horse. I remember him telling us as we followed behind the horse not to get too near as he had fed the horse with turnips that day and I am sure what the consequences of that would be.

TARNS HOUSE

The house that is now called Muirtown House was called Tarns House and stands at the end of Charleston Place. In the 1960's there was a road that ran from the bottom of Firthview Drive past the house and followed what is now Firthview Road to its junction with King Brood Road. The road turned left to what is now the roundabout onto Clachhaharry Road. At the bottom of King Brood Road stood two pillars on top of which were two lions. This was known as the Lions Gates and it was the entrance gate to Tarns House. The local people would tell the children to go to the gates at midnight and said that when the lions heard the town clock they would swap pillars.

I remember that, as it made its way to the house, both sides of the drive were covered with rhododendrons and shrubs. At the bottom of the grounds of the estate opposite the Toll house is a well which is now covered up. There is a wall opposite the Toll house and this was the boundary of the grounds of the Tarns estate.

BLACKPARK BIKES

The bikes we were given were huge and were designed for very tall adults and were bought by my mother along with just about everything else at Frasers Auction Mart which was on Church Street in Inverness. Of course these bikes were of no use to us as we could not get onto the seat and could not reach the pedals.

This was overcome with the assistance of Stan Williamson's father who would help us to make blocks of wood the same size as the pedals and about four inches thick which were bolted to the pedals to shorten the distance to our short legs. We then needed to push the bike to a convenient wall or dike so we could reach the seat and learn to cycle. These bikes usually had three gears and were a long way from the lightweight bikes of today. They are now collectors' items.

HOT WATER BOTTLES

When we stayed with our Grandparents at Elgol on Clachnaharry Road winter nights could be cold. There was none of your modern central heating and in the morning the work of Jack Frost could be see on the windows. The stone Hot Water Bottle was one solution but as there was only one it could not help us all. Then there was the problem of someone kicking this bottle out of bed when it got cold. The noise of it crashing to the floor would wake the whole house.

My mother had the solution to the lack of bottles. She may have found the solution in that old standby for things such as home made jam that would not set, or the address to send to for that certain shade of wool or button - The Peoples Friend. She would take a Hays or a Mackintoshes Lemonade Bottle and fill it with hot water. These lemonade bottles at that time had a screw top. To stop the bottles cracking with the heat a metal knitting needle was put into the bottle as the water was poured. After this a sock was wrapped round the bottle and we were ready for bed.

THE MESSAGE BOY

I worked as a message boy for Wullie Ross who owned the shop at the top of Telford Street, this was about 1960. My mother spoke to Mr Ross about a job for me when I was eleven years old. He was not supposed to start me until I was twelve years old, but I was tall and he gave me a part-time job as a message boy working from 4 to 6 pm, Wednesday to Friday and all day Saturday. There wasn't much choice as we needed the money which was 25 shilling a week plus tips. My mother took or was given one pound and I was left with 5 shillings from my wages.

Message bikes came in different sizes. Mine had a standard rectangular frame at the front to take a large basket. These bikes were used by the butchers and bakers. Sometimes the messages would be in a large box used for eggs and would be so heavy that when the box was put into the frame the back wheel of the bike would come off the ground. The weight of the box would made the bike difficult to steer and it would have to be pushed uphill. I don't remember how I got the box off at the other end as, when my weight was taken off the bike as I got off, the back wheel would lift off the ground again. There was a delivery from Muirtown to Dell Road in Hilton. The box was tiny and would hardly fit on the bike. I didn't like this job and couldn't understand why the customer couldn't carry the messages home in a bag, and of course no tip.

I would sometimes meet Alick who worked for Bell's the butcher which was beside the Black Bull Pub (now the Waterfront). The shop was demolished and the area redeveloped. Alick would tell me had had just come from the slaughterhouse with two buckets of blood which the butcher used to make black puddings. In his hand he had a brown paper package he was delivering to a house on Telford Street. The package contained sausages and Alick had helped himself to two of them. I could see the tops of the sausages sticking out the top of Alick's jacket like two cigars. Alick told me the two sausages were for his tea and asked me if I would like a couple to take home. I declined his kind offer because if Alick continued to give the customer's sausages away he would arrive at the door with nothing.

For those who are too young to know what a message bike looks like you will see Mr. Macleod the gardener using one to transport his tools round Inverness as he goes about his business. A hardy soul, working in all weathers, using a wooden box on the frame of his bike to carry his tools and, yes, a trailer which he tows behind. I believe Mr Macleod has extended his business and taken on another employee who uses another message bike. This may not seem unusual but they both look as if they are in their sixties if not older.

Mr Macleod has been in business in Inverness for some years and has been successful. This shows how success can come without the use of cars or vans but with a lot of hard work.

THE CLACH SCHOOL

Clachnaharry School still stands on the High Street on the right hand side before the Clachnaharry Inn. It is now used as offices.

When I was about six years old I attended the school and was upset. As it was my first day, Miss Macfadden the teacher would hold me up to the rear window and I would watch as the steam train passed heading north. At that time there was a Railway Station at Clachnaharry and a platform. The old Station House still stands and is the home of Davy Andrew who worked for British Waterways along side my uncle George Anderson.

At about 12.30 when we were immersed in our English lessons wondering why drawing pins were pronounced drorring pins and why envelopes were called onvolopes, a roar would be heard coming across the playground calling for Alick and Ian to come home as their dinner was ready. This was Rod Mackenzie calling his boys home to be fed. They would look at Phadgy and she would nod her head and they would go home to eat. They lived at No 9 High Street on the right hand side before the school.

We stayed at school for dinner or, as it is called today, lunch. The food was delivered in insulated metal containers and served by the dinner lady Mrs. Innes.The staff knew that the school dinner was a main source of food for a child of the 1950s or '60s as most people at that time were not very well off and would allow us to go up for second and even third helpings of food. The people who sent the food were sending more food than was needed to the school and at the end of the sitting Mrs. Innes would ask myself and Donald Fraser to flush the soup left in the metal container down the toilet. She said that if the container was returned with food in it, the next time there would be less in the container. Also she was not allowed to give the pupils any unused food to take home and it was with regret that she would ask us to dump liquid food down the toilet when she knew that it could be used in the local homes. But this ensured that when the containers arrived they were full of food and there was plenty for everyone.

At Clachnaharry School we received a good education from Phadgy (Miss Macfadden) and Toshuck (Miss Mackintosh). I would play with Donald Fraser whose mother Mary and his father Simon and Donald's brother Simon lived on the top road above Clachnaharry which leads to Delmore in the house owned by the Forestry Commission. Donald's father was a forestry worker in the Craig Phadrig

Forest above Clachnaharry. I always knew Donald was clever as he would try and explain something to me and I would not be able to understand.

Donald became an engineer and worked on bridges in the highlands including the Kessock Bridge, the Cromarty Bridge, the Kylskue Bridge and, the last I heard, he was going to work in Taiwan to continue his bridge building. Donald was awarded the OBE a few years ago. I searched the pages of the Inverness Courier at the time but couldn't find my own name on the list.

Many a happy day I spent with Donald setting rabbit snares and nearly breaking our necks flying down the forest tracks on a home made bogey made from the wheels of a pram and a fish box.

Back row.
GRAHAM URQUHART. T. BLAKE. SANDY FRASER. P. BLAKE. JOHN BIRD. SIMON FRASER. S. BLAKE. RAYMOND SUTHERLAND. ROBERT BIRD. SANDY PHILIPS
Middle row ALLAN DIGENCE. ALICK MACKENZIE. WATTY PHILIPS. ELIZABETH BIRD. SHEILA MURRAY. ANGELA HARRISON. ALBERT PHILIPS. DONALD FRASER. JAMES MAC GILLIVARY. BLAKE JOHN MACLEOD.
Middle row HELEN MACDONALD. AILEIN JUNOR. SHENDA MACDONALD. FLORENCE SUTHERLAND. AILEEN BROWN. HAZEL URQUHART. ANNABELLE FRASER. FAITH GRANT. HELEN MACRAE. MOIRA JOHNSTONE. JEAN SMITH. HEATHER MURRAY. BERYL ANDERSON.
Front row STEWART NESBIT. DAVID MACDONALD. ? BLAKE. EDNA INNES. BRIAN MACLEOD. ISOBEL MORRISON. IAN MACKENZIE.

Taken at the time of the Queen's Jubilee in 1953 in the centre on the front row are my cousins James and Beryl. On the right hand side are Phadgy [Miss Macfadden] and on the right hand side is [Toshack] Miss Mackintosh.

THE QUILT

After The Second World War there was surplus equipment and clothing and sales took place where just about anything from a lorry to an inflatable life raft could be bought.

I believe the life raft made a very good paddling pool. There was a large surplus of uniforms and a favourite form of bedding was the army coat. The coat was heavy and was put over the blankets to give some extra warmth. Here is a story about an army coat.

Mrs Mackay had three children, Jimmy, Jocky and Wullie. One day she was entertaining one of her neighbours and they were drinking tea in the living room while the boys were playing at trampolines on the beds upstairs. The living room door burst open and in ran Jimmy. His mother asked him what was wrong and Jimmy said, "it's Wullie Ma, he's torn the arm off the army coat". When the visitor had left, Mrs Mackay got her boys together and told them not to let people know that they were using army coats for bedding but to say it was a quilt.

The next week Mrs Mackay was entertaining and the minister and herself were drinking tea in the living room and the boys were jumping up and down on the beds.

Suddenly the living room door burst open and in ran Wullie, his mother asked him what was the matter and Wullie replied, "It's Jimmy, Ma, he's torn the other arm off the quilt."

PORRIDGE IN THE DRAWER

Porridge and oatmeal have been the staple diet of Scots for centuries. Oats are quite hardy and will thrive on not too fertile soil and put up with our, at times, inclement weather. This food is now thought to be very good for us and can reduce our cholesterol levels.

Up until quite recent times it was not uncommon in country areas to make a large pot of porridge at the weekend to use the following week. This was done by pouring the porridge into the top drawer of the kitchen or dining room dresser. It would be marked in squares and would be used as required. It could be reheated when a person came home in the evening. It could be fried or it could be topped with jam and eaten as a sweet. It could be wrapped up and given to a child to take to school and as the week wore on it could be used to feed the dog. At the end of the week the whole process would begin again.

My friend Woody told me that previous generations in Easter Ross would be sent to school with a piece consisting of rolled oats soaked in whisky to see them through the day. Lillian Beckwith tells in her stories of the Hebrides of a man who ate no other food but porridge all his life and showed no signs of ill health. A workmate of mine at Macdermotts yard at Ardersier told me that the closest he came to first hand evidence of porridge in the drawer was when he lived at Betty Hill in the far north of Scotland. As a child he went to a friend's house on the way home. When they got there the boy's mother was not at home but she had left a note for her son. The note said, "I have gone to the shop. I will be back soon. Your dinner is in the drawer."

Another use of porridge was to use it as a poultice to draw a boil. I have had this treatment for a boil on my neck. The poultice is put on as hot as possible and I can tell you that is something to bring a tear to your eye. You don't see children with boils these days. We were probably lacking in vitamins.

HAIR CUTS

When we were children we lived with our grandparents who stayed at Elgol which is on Clachnaharry Road. As money was always short we would be sent along the road to a neighbour, Mr. Third, who would practice his hairdressing skills on us. His tools were very basic and would consist of a hand operated hair trimmer, a pair of scissors and a bowl which was normally used for cooking. A lot of the hair was pulled out by the trimmers and every haircut looked the same. The cooking bowl was put on the head and he would use it as a guide as he cut the hair to the same length. Of course as the old joke goes the difference between a good haircut and a bad haircut is about a week.

As we grew older we were sent to the barber shop owned by Duncy Holmes whose shop stood on the corner of Queens Street and Huntly Street. This area has been re-developed and is now Falconer Court. Duncy Holmes Barber Shop was not like The Salon as seen on the TV. It had a large chair in front of a large mirror and if a child came in for a haircut a wooden board would be placed across the arms of the chair to bring the child up to a suitable height.

Haircuts in the early 1950s were military style haircuts, that is, short back and sides and loads of Brylcream plastered on the top. My brother Watty said that it did not matter if you said no when asked if you wanted Brylcream as he plastered it on anyway.

About this time I was getting a bit fed up of these old fashioned haircuts. The latest haircut was from America and was called a Crew Cut and on my next visit to Duncy Holmes I asked for one. Fair play to Duncy he took the lot off. The looks I got from my Mother, my Granny and my Aunties when I arrived home made me think that they thought there was something drastically wrong with me and that possibly I was not the full shilling. Such was the attitude in the early 1950s to anyone who did not conform to the norm.

As they say, history will repeat itself and in the 1970s our son Andrew arrived home with the latest haircut at that time called Tramlines. He would be about twelve years old and my wife Frances and I were ready to go out for the evening. Andrew was to be dropped off at his Granny's. The effect on myself and Frances as Andrew arrived home with this unusual hair cut was the same as the effect I had on my family when I arrived home with my unusual haircut and we both wondered about the sanity of our son.

I may add that Frances was crying and the whole episode ruined our night out. Although it seemed important at the time it meant nothing and Andrew grew up to be a normal human being and of course I grew up to be a fairly normal human being.

To get back to Duncy Holmes, as he completed a haircut on one of his adult male customers he would ask him if he required anything for the weekend. The younger generation may not understand what this means. The purchase of contraceptives by males was not very straightforward. A young male might enter a chemist shop intending to purchase a packet of Durex (condoms) and when faced by a young female assistant would ask for a packet of aspirin or yet another packet of throat pastilles and when he found that his bathroom cabinet was full of medication he did not need he would take the barber up on his offer. Something For The Weekend would be discreetly slipped into the customer's hand with his change thereby saving him the embarrassment of facing that young girl at the chemist shop. The modern condom vending machine has thankfully put a stop to our dependence on the barber to supply contraceptives.

The only question is why the weekend was thought to be the time when contraceptives were required but we won't go into that, or, as they say nowadays, we don't want to go there.

FOOD

When I was a child food was in short supply and nothing was wasted. Today dieticians say that after the war the nation was at its most healthy. Meals consisted of plain but wholesome foods such as porridge, mince and tatties, broth and other soups, stovies, macaroni, rice and stew.

Another reason for our health was that we did not have computers and television to keep us indoors and would spend most of the day finding things to amuse ourselves, such as making a tree swing or a bow and arrows, or making a coracle out of tree branches and a piece of tarpaulin, or fishing for flukies in the estuary at the back of the canal in the sea, and fishing for brown trout, sea trout and the elusive salmon in the canal.
I must not forget the Burnetts Plain Loaf which was a main part of the diet. The heel of the loaf was keenly sought after as it was thicker than the rest of the loaf. It had a waxy finish to it and was delicious toasted. I remember my mother talking to a woman who lived at the top of Hawthorn Drive discussing the Burnetts loaf. The woman said that they threw away the heels but that she would save them for her. This may seem hard to believe when we see the food that is wasted today but that is how it was in the 1950s.

My friend Woody who came from Easter Ross told me that when he was a child they would have chicken stew for their dinner until they found a piece of lead shot in the dinner and they realised that they were eating rabbit. I can also remember my Grand-Father Albert Gibson remarking to my Granny that if he continued to have boiled eggs every night for his tea he would be ashamed to look a chicken in the a---.
As the days shortened and autumn replaced summer and all those Inverness people with what is thought to be a very pure English were saying, "aye the nights are fair drawing in", our thoughts would turn to the large gardens and orchards in the area. We would watch as the fruit ripened on the branches as we

51

passed and waited our opportunity to organise what was called a raid on a garden which would take place after dark.

We were staying with our Grandparents at Elgol on Clachnaharry Road. Behind this house was a field and a wall about twelve feet high behind which was the orchard for Clachnaharry House which at that time was the home of the manager of the Caledonian Canal. My brother Watty and our neighbour Jimmy Fraser spotted a branch from a tree inside the orchard on the outside of the wall and Jimmy was standing on Watty's shoulders and picking fruit from the tree when the gardener opened a door in the orchard wall and caught them red handed. Jimmy started crying and pleaded with the man not to tell his father as it would mean that he would get a terrible hammering. They heard no more about it. In those days a hefty skelp on the lug was never far away.

As I go about my business in Inverness today the fruit trees can be touching the ground with the amount of fruit they carry. I can assure you that in the 1950s that would not happen.

PLUM DUFF (CHRISTMAS PUDDING)

This was a pudding made for Christmas. I do not have a recipe but it included mixed fruit, cinnamon, eggs, flour, etc. It was supposed to include silver sixpences. It was mixed in a large bowl and covered in flour which gave it a skin and was put inside a large cloth and steamed in a pan until it was cooked.

I spoke to a workmate of mine called Mick who was brought up in Glasgow who told me that their plum duff was cooked in a pillow case. He came from a very large family and this pudding was designed to last many days after Christmas and nobody ever found the elusive Silver Sixpences. This was not because they had eaten them but because they had never been added; it was to encourage the children to continue to eat the pudding and to make sure there was no waste. When the pudding was a few days old it could be fried; I have tasted this and it is delicious.

MAM'S SOUP

My mother-in-law Rita Ruxton made some wonderful meals when we stayed at her home in the 1970s.

A favourite was her soup which she made using a piece of sirloin beef. She had learned to make this in the kitchen of some large house when she was young. She told me that the reason for the uniform exact small square size of the turnip and carrots came from her training in these kitchens as she said that if they were not of the required size a hand would give you the usual skelp on the lug.

The soup was served and you were supposed to sup or eat the bree, that is the liquid from the soup, and leave the vegetables to be accompanied by the beef which was sliced and added to the soup when it had cooled. To this was added a dry tatty such as a Kerr's Pink. As an accompaniment, a Meally Jimmy was served, that is, a white pudding, bought from one of the now rare family butchers now in business in Inverness.

If you have the time to make this today, which is doubtful, I recommend it as a wholesome and delicious meal. Excuse my fascination with food but it comes from a time when we were always looking for more and we were young and trying to grow fast.

PANCAKES

Seven table-spoons of self raising flour
One pinch of salt
One dessert spoon of sugar
One egg
One small teaspoon of baking powder
One tea- spoon of syrup
A knob of margarine or butter
A cup of milk

Melt the syrup and the margarine
Slowly beat eggs and sugar together.
Mix flour salt and milk in a large bowl or jug.
Add the melted syrup and margarine to a nice dropping consistency.
Finally add the baking powder.
The mixture should drop slowly from a spoon.
Leave to stand before using.

The secret of good pancake making is the temperature of the pan or girdle in use.
A large or medium cast-iron frying pan can be used and a low to medium heat is required.
Drop tablespoons or cover the whole frying pan with the mix. The pan should be lightly greased with butter before using.
When the pancake mix shows broken bubbles on top it is time to turn over.
Cook the second side for two to three minutes then turn out onto a wire tray to cool.
Or serve warm with butter or jam.

There you have it. The old family recipe for pancakes. You can add more or less sugar or salt to suit your taste. The more sugar you add the more the pancakes will rise .

THE BLACK BULL

The Black Bull is now The Waterfront Pub and Restaurant on Huntly Street. Behind the bar in the Black Bull hanging on the wall was a stuffed black bull's head complete with large horns.

I was told that once, a game of darts was in progress and one person was down to 50. Instead of continuing the game and ending on a double the person on 50 asked the other player if he would accept Bull for the game. The bull's eye on a dartboard is worth 50 points and it was agreed that if the bull was hit the game was won. But what the player trying for the bull did was throw a dart and hit the bull's head behind the bar and tried to claim the game.

THE CYCLOPS

This is a story told to me by that expert storyteller Lindsey Redford (The Driver) who worked with me at Mcdermotts at Ardersier.

Jimmy, Jocky and The Driver were drinking in the Black Bull one Saturday morning. By about 2.30 they had had enough to drink. The Driver said, 'where's Jocky?' he had not been seen for some time and was not in the bar. They thought he had wandered off and made his way home to the Ferry where he lived. The Ferry is the large housing estate beside the Kessock Ferry Road. So The Driver and Jimmy walked down to the Ferry and went to Jocky's house and knocked on the door. There was no answer and the door was open so they went into the kitchen and found Jocky. He had made himself a big fry-up of bacon, egg, black pudding, sausage and fried bread but due to the large amount of drink Jocky had drunk at the Bull he had collapsed and he was face down in his plate.

The Driver told me that his friend Jimmy got a terrible fright. When the Driver pulled Jocky back into his chair the fried egg had stuck to Jocky's forehead. Jimmy thought he was one of those Cyclops, you know the monster with the one eye in the middle of its forehead. The Driver told me he had a terrible job convincing Jimmy it wasn't a Cyclops but only Jocky with a fried egg stuck to his forehead. The Driver said it was a true story.

DOUBLE TAKE

This story won a competition in a fishing magazine which I entered last year. The prize was a bottle of 21-year-old whisky and a hip flask.

I have fished for some forty odd years and can remember only once catching two fish on one fly. Anglers have caught two and sometimes three fish on a three-fly cast, but two fish on one fly? My friend John Fraser and I had the privilege of fishing in the evening on Loch Mhuillidh in Strathfarrer, which is in the Highlands north of Beauly. I was casting from the boat when I hooked a brown trout of about half a pound. Then there was a movement on the surface. I thought a trout had taken another fly on the cast. But as I played the trout we could see a jack pike of about half a pound had attacked it and refused to let it go. John netted the two fish and we could see the pike with its jaw locked onto the back of the trout, and when the two fish were knocked on the head we could see a vee cut into the back of the trout, cutting half way through the flesh. Yes, two fish on one fly and a witness to boot.

SALMON NETTING ON THE RIVER NESS

There is a part of the River Ness called the Friars Shott. This name is thought to go back to early Inverness when the Friars had the fishing rights to this part of the river. When I was a boy in the nineteen fifties my family would picnic on the bank of the river in front of the Black Bull and myself and my brothers would swim in the river. At that time the salmon fishers would cast their nets across the river then row their fishing cobbles across and pull the net onto the shore. We would see the salmon and sea-trout they netted as the fish migrated from the sea to Loch Ness and beyond. This practice has long since disappeared because of the scarcity of fish due to over-fishing and the returning fish being caught on the high seas by trawlers etc.

As a boy in the nineteen fifties I can remember watching the local anglers catching huge salmon in the higher reaches of the River Ness. The pool I am writing about was one of the best pools on the Inverness Angling Club waters - the Macintyre Pool. I can remember a local angler heading home with a salmon tied to the handlebars of his bike; the fish's tail was touching the ground. This fish would have been over thirty pounds in weight, not an uncommon occurrence and fish of heavier weights were caught.

Getting back to my story in front of the Black Bull. We were swimming in the River Ness and the Salmon Fishing cobbles were working their nets. My brother Watty was swimming beside the boat when he got into difficulties and was about to be swept down-river when he was spotted by one of the fishermen and pulled to safety. He was taken onto the river bank and resuscitated and would have drowned if the fisherman had not spotted him.

This Postcard captures the scene exactly as it would have been in the nineteen-fifties. Note the boys swimming beside the Salmon Fishing cobles.

Netting salmon on the river Ness at Friar's Shott.
On the right is Donnie Maclean.
In the background to the left of the Black Bridge is "Hill 60"
and to the right is the destructor where refuse used to be incinerated,
providing hot water for the local swimming baths next door.

ODE TO CLACHNAHARRY

The 'Cappie Brae' is white with snow
So a sledging we must go
With wooly gloves and hats so cosy
Our cheeks and noses they look rosy
Down the brae we slide so fast
We hit the bottom with a bump
Must have hit an old tree stump
Jock the joiner made the sledge
Mustn't go near Granda Innes's hedge
There's old Mrs Kintrea the bone setter
Where we go to "make things better"
Young Willuk and Jimma are off on the bus
To get the old lady's ounce of snuff
Old Mrs Wood with her pooper scooper
Not a trace of hen's dirt --- just super.
Jimmy Gunn in the signal box
Forever polishing the brass and clocks
Dan MacKay the blacksmith lights the forge
Someone shouts "Hurry, there's uncle George"
Kenny MacLean the canal diver
Every dip he made paid less than a fiver
Alistair Cadenhead canal carpenter rare
You should see his cartoons they are beyond compare
Willie Mason with his camping park
All the Glaswegians came for a lark
His brother's bike handlebars laden with rabbits
Made the poor man a wee bit crabbit
Jess and Nat they had the inn
Many a Clacher left there in a spin
Tom MacHardy with his cheery smile
Sold petrol to take cars many a mile

Davy Andrew "now that's your man" and
His wife Alice have you tasted her jam?
The Bill Thirds they live in "Quirang"
Got many a chase their door bell we rang
Mr Owens he mended bikes
Don't think he tried his hand with trikes
Jock thepainter "before the roller"
His famous last words were"nice warm colour"
Bob Collins he lived with Jess and Frank
He thought he was one of the upper rank
That other boy Gunn we all called 'Bing'
Far up the Rockies we could hear him sing
"There's a train coming" we'd all scream
Then a mad rush to the top of the bridge for steam
Remember that little house called the "Neuk"?
Its garden was always worth a second look
Who couldforget oldBobbuk Thompson
With his sister Nell he was never lonesome
Margaret and Lena MacKenzie (nee)
Where do they get their eternal youth?
Delightfulpeople and that's the truth
The Greigs lived opposite the school
"Perfection in dress" their golden rule
Jess and Ian MacLeod had theonly shop
Selling highland toffee and cough drops
Old Jean 'Donald at "the gala" was there
Her penny farthing bike got many a stare
The Christies sold the paraffin
They filled our bottles from a tin
TheSimon MacDonalds lived in "Dunolly"
That's where we went to steal their holly
The MacLennans lived next to the shop
Son Victor went toGlasgow to be a cop

The Jamieson family lived near by
I believe their son 'Bonto' does a good 'fly tie'
We'd better not forget old "Jock the post"
Or we may be haunted with his ghost
Willie MacKay has seen a few summers
His wifeDoris the first incomer
Under the 'Cartuck tree' they all met
Pipes stuffed with "Bogie Roll" and all matches spent
The toll house now has changed a bit
Willie and Angie McRae wouldn't know it
Alec MacLean canal gardene rtook pride
In making bouquets for the brides
Jock Murray's clan came from "the Glasgow fair"
All his parties "were a tare"
Bengie the coalman, the man we could not live without
He radiates warmth without a doubt
We'd walk out to MacGruers farm
No tmany cars to do us harm
Up to the poultry farm with tired legs
We paid a sixpence for the chipped eggs
Simon Fraser "Craig Phadrig" we were told to see
He always gave us our Christmas tree
To us all the sealock is a picture
Forever in our minds --- a fixture
The smellof "the culb" made us groan
We really thought it was "Ozone"
Len and Albert Philips and cousin Beryl true Clachers born
BrothersWalter Sandy and Rob ar Invernessian's sworn
Look out when the Gibsons and Birds are about
"They are related" I heard someone shout
Albert Gibson with hislovely smile
Which kept his 6 Gibson girls in line

Good Luck to all Clachers in 1997
Ann Philips (nee Gibson)

At one time there were three distilleries in Inverness producing whisky; today all that remains are the buildings now used as a hotel and restaurant on Millburn Road.

This was once the Millburn Distillery. the other two were the Glen Mhor Distillery and the Glen Albyn Distillery at Muirtown. The Glen Albyn Distillery stood on what is now the B+Q store and the Glen Mhor Distillery is now the car park for the Retail Park on Telford Street. The Glen Mhor had its own coopers who made the barrels or casks.

I have a miniature barrel made by the coopers in the 1970s; it holds about a gallon. Sadly it holds only water at present. The water swells the staves and holds the barrel together by swelling the joints.If it is allowed to dry, the staves contract and the barrel falls apart. The distilleries were owned by Mackinlays and Birnie Ltd. Mr. Birnie was the Provost of Inverness.

There is an interesting story about The Glen Albyn Distillery. There was a pipe laid from the spirit safe along the quayside at Muirtown Wharf to what was the Muirtown Hotel. This is the building now converted into flats across the road from the shop at the top of Telford Street. This meant that the hotel had a supply of whisky at no charge. The person who laid the pipe emigrated to Australia and on his return a few years later informed the Custom and Excise that there was an illegal pipe in place. This resulted in the Distillery losing its license for some time.

A spirit safe is a brass and glass cabinet containing hydrometers to check the specific gravity of the spirit as it pumped from the still to the spirit tanks where it is stored. The spirit safe is padlocked and sealed and the hydrometers are raised and lowered by levers on the outside of the safe. One can be seen in the foyer of the Thistle Hotel on Millburn Road.

In the picture I took about 1980 showing the G. L. (The Gate-Lifter) which was used to move the lock gates for the Caledonian Canal, the buildings on the right hand side were the warehouses used to store the whisky as it matured. When the casks were being moved from the warehouse the excise man would attend to see that there was no pilfering. But this did not stop the distillery workers. The workers would use what was known as a Dog. This was a piece of copper tube about an inch in diameter and about 12 inches long with an old copper penny soldered onto one end. On the other end two lugs were attached and a piece of string was attached to the lugs. It had a cork to seal it when it was full. The Dog was hidden down a trouser leg. When the look-out was in place keeping an eye on the excise-man the worker would remove the bung from the cask and lower the dog by the string and fill it and cork it and hide it down his trouser leg and replace the bung in the cask.

The other container used was a copper tank formed to the shape of the lower stomach and hidden inside the top of the trousers. The worker had a length of small diameter tube in his pocket and when the bung was removed he used the tube to siphon off about three pints of matured whisky into the tank. The tank would be taken from inside the trousers and laid on the ground. This would help the siphoning because of the different levels between the cask and the floor. Care had to be taken when this was happening as any spillage would give the game away. The tank was put on the cinder path which ran along the side of the casks so any spillage would disappear into the cinders and not be seen.

Pilfering from casks of matured whisky was difficult to detect as the longer a cask of whisky is matured the more the whisky evaporates and the contents diminish. So everyone got their share even the Angels. The Angels share is the cloud of condensed vapour seen as steam coming from a chimneystack when a distillery is producing whisky. This can be seen in the distilleries that are still in production all over Scotland and which are well worth a visit.

Sadly the Angels Share can no longer be seen in Inverness. At the time of the closing of the two distilleries at Muirtown in the late 1970s the warehouses at the Glen-Albyn Distillery held 2,000,000 gallons of whisky not to mention the amount of whisky stored in the bonded warehouses in the Glen-Mhor Distillery. Both distilleries were capable of producing a total of 600,000 gallons of whisky in a season between them - that's an awful amount of drams. Most of the whisky produced was used to blend other whiskies but the distillery produced a ten-year-old malt whisky called Glen-Mhor (Mhor means Great in Gaelic).

A season was only part of a year because when temperatures fluctuated in the summer it made temperature control more difficult and this is vital to distilling whisky.

So for part of the year the distilleries were shut down for maintenance. The water used in the Muirtown Distilleries came from Loch Ness via a pipe which ran from the Top Lock of The Caledonian Canal and down the canal bank to the distilleries. I was told that no pumps were involved in assisting the flow of the water and it was gravity fed. As the temperature of the water is important in the production of whisky the distilleries had an advantage when using water from loch as the temperature of the water varies by only one or two degrees from summer to winter. This is probably due to the vast amount of water which Loch Ness holds.

There is one thing my family are grateful for, and that is the closing of the Muirtown Distilleries in the late 1970s as it probably saved the life of my brother Watty Philips who worked in the Distilleries from the age of seventeen. If he had continued to work as a stillman he would have died quite young. This is because of the amount of whisky consumed by the distillery workers. Twice a day they would be given a large dram by their employer, one in the morning and one in the afternoon. The workers would also drink the raw spirit after it was distilled. This was known as The Clearuck, clear spirit between 120 and 130 proof. This was chased down with some lemonade.

Of course The Health and Safety at Work Act put a stop to all this and today we find it hard to believe that an employer would give alcohol to his employees during working hours and not realise the effect this could have on their safety.

A HEART WARMING STORY

My brother Watty Philips was working on the night shift at the Glen-Albyn Distillery. This would be in the late nineteen sixties.

At the break for lunch during the shift Watty took an Alsatian dog belonging to a work mate for a walk along the Canal Banks which were behind the distillery. As he left the rear of the distillery by a gate that led to the canal banks he saw a man beside the heap of coal which was used to fire the furnaces used to flavour the malt prior to whisky making.

He asked the man what he was doing and the man said he was filling a small bag with coal from the heap. It was Christmas Eve and it was very cold. The man said he came from Cameron Square which was not far from the distillery and he needed some coal for his fire as he did not want his children to wake up in the morning on Christmas Day to a cold house.

Watty told the man to stay where he was and he went back into the distillery and returned with a grain sack and some string. A grain sack is about six feet long and about three feet wide. Watty doubled the sack to make a sack of about three feet by three feet.

He helped the man to fill the sack with coal and tied the top of the sack with string. He then helped the man to load the sack onto his bike. It was a ladies bike and had no crossbar. The sack was loaded onto the frame.

Watty then helped the man to push the bike to the top of the steps leading to the Carse area of the Merkinch from the canal bank and they both guided the load down the steps and the man pushed the bike to his home at Cameron Square. Before leaving, the man thanked Watty for his kindness and Watty told him to come back on the following Sunday night shift and he would get a sack of peat.

The man's name was Mr Stewart and his children would now be it their forties. If any one reading this story remembers a Christmas holiday with roaring fires and the aroma of the peat reek they had their fuel courtesy of Watty Philips and the Whisky Distillers Mackinlay and Birnie.

A distillery worker clears snow as the sun rises on a winter's morning.

This photo was taken from the rear of the Glen-Mhor Distillery looking across the Carse area of the Merkinch as it was in the 1970s. The Kessock Bridge is still under construction at the top right hand side of the photo.

The Glen Mhor Distillery before it was demolished.

This view is taken from the bottom lock of Muirtown Locks. All that now remain are ivy cottage in the centre and the shop at the top of Telford Street.

THE CLACH PUB AND THE PAINTER

This Yarn took place about thirty years ago. A local painter had the job of painting the toilets and the poolroom of the Clachnaharry Inn one afternoon when the pub was closed. The pub owner, George Maclean, and my brother Sandy Philips had gone to play golf and had left the painter to get on with the painting. What they did not understand was the temptation this worker was under as he looked along the optic gallery at all those drams behind closed doors and with no supervision.

When the golfers returned in the late afternoon to get the pub ready for opening at five o'clock, they were in for a bit of a surprise. When they opened the door they found a painter lying in a heap on the floor and there was yellow paint everywhere. There were yellow hand prints on the glasses on the bar, there was yellow paint on the floor and when his handiwork was inspected in the pool room, it was found that he had painted over the posters on the walls and had continued painting over the windows in the pub toilets. I was told that the yellow colour scheme continued outside the pub as the painter's yellow footprints could be seen on the pavement outside as he staggered home.

I believe that was the last painting job this painter did for George Maclean.

My brother Sandy was told that the unusual round stone built into the wall at the front of the Clachnaharry Inn was used as a stop for the wheel of a coach or a cart to stop it rolling backwards. Since he told me that I have noticed similar stones in and on other old buildings. I can remember the steel tethering rings on the wall of the front of the Inn. They were beside the shutters.

THE ROCKIES

In the 1950s a family of travelling people lived behind the Monument in Clachnaharry known locally as the Rockies. They had a small caravan in which the women and children lived. The men and the older boys slept outside in the open under a tarpaulin tent or a bendy tent supported by branches from a tree.
I can remember Jimmy Fraser, who was a member of this family, telling me that the rats would run over them as they slept.

Jimmy was a great footballer and had a trial for Caley (Inverness Caledonian Football team). We played our football in a field which is now Swanson Avenue. If Jimmy won the ball you could forget about getting it back.
Jimmy attended Inverness High School and would run from the Rockies to school but not before washing at the Priseag Well (pronounced Preeshuck). This well was at the side of the Beauly road about fifty yards past the railway bridge on the left hand side of the road. At one time this well was the water supply for the village of Clachnaharry and many trips would have been made to this well by local people before they had piped water.

The water from this well was excellent and was thought to have curative powers. If someone was in hospital recovering from illnes, a bottle of water from the Priseag Well was taken to them. The well disappeared about ten years ago though it seems a pity it was removed. The water came from somewhere in the hills above in the vicinity of Craig Phadrig. The water still comes down the hill but now it runs under the road and onto Clachnaharry beach and we have no access but go to a supermarket to buy a bottle of Spring Water.

LINDA'S STORY

Linda was brought up in Inverness in the Council Housing estate known as the Ferry. Her story took place between 1960 and 1970.

Bath night was on a Sunday; a large metal bath was taken into the living room and filled with water. Linda was fifth out of seven children to be bathed by which time the water was dirty and two more had to use it. One bath a week was normal. I asked Linda why they did not use the public baths on Glebe Street. She said that would cost money and they couldn't afford it. Her father was an alcoholic and drank most of the money.

An alcoholic had a difficult time in the Ferry as there were people who would supply them with alcohol at expensive prices during the week and wait for them as they came out of work with their wages to collect the money. Their first drink was free and an alcoholic could not stop after one drink and would be given more. So by the time Linda's father arrived home on a Friday night there was very little money left.

In the summer Linda would play on the streets of the Ferry but they were taken inside at 7.30 pm even if the sun was shining. The voice of her father would be heard to say: "Right you, in." Linda would plead to be left outside to play. Her father would say that's OK if you can get me an empty lemonade bottle or get me some money for a fag. She hunted for a lemonade bottle and went to the shop and for the empty bottle was given one cigarette which she took home and gave to her father. This meant that she got an extra half hour outside.

Linda would play in the streets with a girl who had blonde hair that was pleated and stretched all the way down her back. Linda would ask the girl how she managed to keep her hair clean as Linda's washing facilities were somewhat basic. The girl said she did not wash her hair. Shortly after this discussion Linda's friend was taken to Raigmore Hospital as she had an infestation of head lice and all her hair was shaved off to remove them. The unfortunate child had to endure the taunts of her fellow pupils at her Primary School next day as she attended wearing a head square to cover her bald head.

Linda told me that the annual washing of the bedding took place in the summer. This was to remove the fleas and bed bugs from the blankets. The metal bath that was used to bathe them was used to wash the blankets. The bath was taken outside and filled with hot water and Linda and her sisters would tramp on the blankets to get them clean. The bedding was then hung out to dry and so the annual ritual was over for another year.

HEATING

Linda's house was heated by a coal fire and I asked Linda if they kept the coal in the bath. I was told that this did happen in the Ferry area because anything of value left outside could be stolen. She said the coal was not kept in the bath as the metal bath was used for bathing and at this time there was no bath in the bathroom. She said the coal was kept in a cupboard under the stairs.

She remembers a time when there was more heat in the house than usual. Her father got a job in a saw mill and when he returned home at night he would have two sacks of sawdust on each handlebar of his bike. This was to burn with small bag of coal, which they bought from the local shop, and with the pram full of cinders taken home from the gas works at the bottom of Academy Street. This was from the Gas Boards where coal was used to produce gas for the town of Inverness. The cinders were cheap to buy and were used for paths etc.

Linda remembers the humiliating experience of having to accompany her younger sister along Kessock Road with the family's usual form of transport (the pram) to the Gas Board premises at the bottom of Academy Street to collect cinders for the fire. Linda said the coat her sister was wearing was a mustard colour with large pink buttons. I think Linda was more embarrassed by her sister's fashion sense than by the fact that they were pushing an empty pram along the street.

The fire would need some form of kindling to get it started and Linda said this was done by pulling twigs from the local trees and drying them indoors until they could be used.

THE FAMILY HEIRLOOMS

Linda and her siblings were moved to another house in the Ferry. Their father was left on his own. Linda said the Welfare (The Social Services) gave them beds and bedding and some cutlery and pans for the new house.

Linda's mother said there was some blue and white china which belonged to her in the old house and asked Linda and her sister go round for it. They were not very keen as they were frightened of their father. Linda's mother said not to worry as the B------ would be sleeping. They were told to take the pram. So they headed off to try and get the china for their mother.

When they got to the house the door was not locked and they crept up the stairs to the living room and sure enough the B------ was asleep on the couch surrounded by his empty beer tins. They crept past him into the kitchen and were making their way to the top of the stairs when he woke up. They ran for it and made it to the bottom of the stairs and put the china in the pram and ran down the street to their father shouting abuse about their mother as they ran away. And so the Family Heirlooms were retained.

THE CHIP VAN

Linda told me that once she had been sent out to get a sixpenny bag of chips from the chip van which parked on the large roundabout on Kessock Avenue. Note that this sixpence worth of chips was supposed to feed seven children. As Linda went towards the chip van a girl from a local family, who Linda called the --- --------, approached her and took the sixpence from her. Linda went home and told her mother what had happened.

When she got home her mother told her that if she did not get the sixpence back from the girl she would get a hammering (beating) when she got home. She went back and confronted the girl and said she wanted her sixpence back as this was the money for the tea. She went out onto the street and fought for the sixpence and won. This would have been no small fight as the family she was fighting had a local reputation for being tough. Linda said she had no choice as she would have had a harder time if she went home without the chips.

When Linda was older she worked in the same chip van. When she saw people as poor as her family approach, she took pity on them and when the owner was not looking she would, as she said, bung them a fish or a black pudding as they ordered their sixpence worth of chips. Or she would say, "and what's that, a bottle of Cola?" The only problem with this was that as the local people worked out when Linda was working in the van the queues would be very long. She did say that when she was working in the van the profits for the owner must have been very small.

BOWL OF MEAL FRASERS

I asked Linda what her maiden name was and she said it was Fraser, but she was not a Bowl of Meal Fraser. What she meant was they were not Boll of Meal Frasers.

After the battle of Culloden the head of the Clan Fraser, Lord Lovat, found that his Clan was somewhat depleted and went round the countryside asking families who were not Frasers to join his Clan. They were offered a Boll of Meal if they accepted. A Boll of Meal was a sack-full of meal weighing 140 pounds and would have fed a family for months and so many took up the offer and became Frasers.

I have been in the company of a person named Fraser who would remark about another Fraser that they were not true Frasers but Boll of Meal Frasers. So the phrase Boll of Meal Frasers has continued from 1745 until the present time.

1960's FASHION

Cuban heeled shoes were the fore-runner of the Platform shoes which are back in fashion again and I suppose that if you never throw anything away it will eventually come back into fashion (remember the Kipper Ties). The Cuban Heel shoe was designed to give the wearer extra height and as I was quite tall I must have looked about seven feet tall. Trousers were flared at the bottom and had turn-ups.

My friend the Driver told me that you had to be very careful when wearing the combination of Cuban heeled shoes and Bell-Bottomed trousers with turn-ups as, if there was a strong wind blowing, a sudden gust could send you staggering sideways and the high heeled Cuban heeled shoe could get caught in the turn-up of your trousers. You would find it very difficult to stop and regain your balance, especially if you were trying to go down a flight of stairs or steps in a dignified fashion.

THE SECRET DIARY OF ALBERT BIRD

Albert Bird was born in Inverness. His family came from Clachnaharry beside the Beauly Firth. When Albert was fourteen years old he was put on a ship which was bound for England. This would be about 1938. It was a very stormy day when Albert left and he was seasick and home sick before he was out of the Beauly Firth.The following pages are from his secret diary which he kept during the Second World War.

The starting date is June 5th 1944. The start of the Invasion of Normandy was June 6th 1944; this was known as D Day. This was the largest Invasion in history and was conducted by British and Allied Forces against Nazi Germany. The invasion could not fail as it would have meant that we today would probably be under the rule of a Dictator. Albert mentions the beachheads he had to visit. The allied invasion beaches were called Sword, Juno, Utah, Gold and Omaha. The American Forces went ashore on Omaha beach and suffered heavy casualties as they tried to move off the beach.

I have a great admiration for those who fought and died in the First and Second World Wars so we could have our freedom. Albert writes of his experiences in a very matter of fact way. The fear he felt as he entered these War Zones must have been very intense and there is no mention of the courage it must have taken to make so many trips to the Normandy Beachheads. Future ceremonies of remembrance will get smaller and smaller as the number of survivors grow fewer in number. Albert is now past four score years and is living with his wife Betty in Aberdeen. Albert served as Coxswain of the Aberdeen Life-boat for many years and I am sure he helped to save many lives from the Sea.

Albert could have written a very interesting biography and I am indebted to Albert for the use of his Diary in my book. Albert's Diary of his experiences during the Normandy Landings will be displayed in the Maritime Museum in London and rightly so.

June 15th 1944 - the date when Albert and his mates may have thought that they had done their bit and arrived back at Southampton Docks they were loaded with a cargo of Octane which I believe is High Octane Fuel to take back to the Americans on Omaha beach.

The use of the mulberry harbour: this was a concrete structure which was taken to the beaches in parts and re-assembled there. In order to do this, a ship had to arrive on the beach at a certain time so the tide could leave the ship high and dry on the beach.

The use of a kedge anchor: this was an anchor which was towed behind the ship on a length of Cable and as the tide lifted the ship off the beach this anchor was used to pull the ship clear of the beach. The Sixtieth Anniversary of D Day took place on 6th June 2004.

Here is Albert's Story...

ALBERT'S STORY

May 1944
Merchant Ship No 461
Requistioned for special duties with a full cargo of war materials
and a voluntary crew sailed from London docks. Destination -
South coast of England. Destination was in fact Southampton
Docks. Without going into details we knew that something big
was about to happen. Southampton was literally bursting at the
seams.
We had a company of soldiers onboard, God knows where they
will be accommodated. Heavy tarpaulins have been stretched
across the derricks above the hatches over the ships holds, so it
looks like this will be it for them until we arrive at where we are
going. Ship now at anchor in the Solent.

June 5th 1944.
Ship put on standby to sail.

June 6th 1944.
Ship No 461.Sailed from Southampton waters in convoy.
Weather very unsettled, moving out into English Channel.
Overcast. Moderate- to- rough sea. Proceeding in convoy. –
Weather not good. A tremendous convoy, Naval and Merchant
Ships, Landing Craft Ships of all sizes and descriptions… A
great sight.
The convoy is heavily escorted by sea and in the air. The
weather is not helping and many of our soldier friends are
suffering from sea-sickness. Sea very rough, vessel rolling quite
heavily, Miserable conditions for these lads…French coast is in
sight. Our orders say "Proceed to Sword Beach, Ouistreham The
most easterly beach.
Anchored off Sword. We heard the battle long before we
reached the beachhead. Very heavy gunfire on shore. Enemy
planes over beach. All ships putting up a heavy barrage. A
tremendous and frightful sight. Worried about our soldiers once

they get ashore – where will they go – They had a miserable crossing.

June 7th 1944.
The battle rages on a few miles inland.

June 8th 1944.
05.00 hrs With daylight in, Enemy air activity slackens.
06.00hrs British fighters overhead, all ships cease fire. Cargo being unloaded all day. Our Battleships resume heavy shelling. Enemy planes over beaches again. Our Lightening and Spitfire planes now in battle over the beaches.
21.00hrs. Formation of enemy planes over beachhead (Bombing) too close for comfort. One of the cargo handling soldiers wounded by machine gun fire from same planes. Bullet through his belly and out again. He will be on his way home soon. Transferred to Hospital ship. Nasty when they start machine gunning the ships.
Midnight. More bombing of beachhead. Usual heavy barrage from ships at anchor.
Air Raids continue most of the night (no sleep)

June 9th 1944.
03.10hrs.Battleships restart shelling coast. Tremendous barrage from the heavy Battleships. Heavy fighting going on ashore.
12.00hrs. Low clouds, heavily overcast today.
17.00hrs. Enemy fighter- bombers over beaches, ships usual heavy flack our only protection. Today very low cloud, no allied aircraft over the area.
23.30hrs. German bombers over in force – not very happy. Bombs too close for comfort.
We have 80 Naval personnel on board for passage to England, having left their ship scuttled at Arromanches, to be used as a block ship. We have no accommodation for them on this ship so it could be an uncomfortable passage home for them. At least they are going back to England.

June 10th 1944.
Dawn Breaking.Enemy planes coming in low over the beachhead, coming in to make their runs singly. Mighty barrage to greet them. I feel much safer behind the guns and I enjoy my stint behind the Orlekon. Visibility very bad this morning. One enemy plane from the last raid will NOT return to base.
The heavy Battleships still hammering the coast. Cargo discharge going well now.

June 10th 1944.
07.00hrs Completed unloading, at last we leave the anchorage at Sword Beach and proceed to join convoy for our passage home. Have to anchor again for a few hours as the roadway is not clear for shipping.
11.00hrs. On our way home. Normandy coast fading away from horizon. Nobody sorry, including our 80 passengers. But sorry for the lads that are left behind.
16.00hrs. A nice smooth passage back to England.
19.00hrs. English coast in sight. Air and Sea escort for convoy all the way home.
21.30hrs – Almost Midnight. Anchor safely in Solent. Watches maintained. Hope for a little sleep. Naval Personnel disembarked. We say goodbye to our Naval friends.

June 11th 1944.
We are still at anchor in Solent, awaiting orders.

June 15th 1944.
Proceed towards Southampton Docks to load Octane – (Oh My God !!)
Managed to have a few words on phone to Mum and dad. But no definite news about my brothers, Magnus, Robert and Peter. Mum thinks Peter is on his way to the Far East and Magnus and Bob are involved in the Normandy Landings.

June 17th 1944.

Few hours ashore today, met my cousin A. Corbett on docks (it's a small world) tried to phone home again but no line available, still I was pleased to see one of my relations so far from home.

June 18th 1944.

We sailed this evening at 2000 hrs for the Cherbourg Peninsular, American beachhead of Omaha.

June 19th 1944.

Am. Sky overcast, Moderate sea, more like a winters day (What has happened to the summer of 1944)

Midday on watch again, Conditions still the same. Not very comfortable.

16.00hrs. nearing |American Omaha beach. Heavy rain-storm, moderate seas, running in on beach.

Midnight. Weather conditions very bad, heavy seas running. Ship rolling moderately. Steam blowers used frequently to clear holds of Octane fumes from leaky containers.

Gunfire a few miles away lighting up the night sky. There will be no chance of unloading cargo in this weather.

04.00hrs. On watch again (A little sleep) Afraid to sleep. Enemy planes over. No bombs on anchorage. Bombing on shore. No change in weather.

12.00hrs. All unloading at a standstill, owing to weather conditions. (God help us please) Sitting on top of 500 tons of High Octane.

16.00hrs. Wind now about gale force, ship not very happy at anchor in these conditions, labouring heavily at anchor. There is nowhere to go – Heavy swell running in on beach. Not a happy time for us.

Midnight. Thank God – No enemy activity. Get rid of this cargo and get home safely again.

June 21st 1944.

04.00hrs.Early signs of dawn, French coast looks very peaceful. Still at anchor, still no chance of being unloaded, but weather seems to be moderating. No enemy aircraft over Omaha thank goodness. Still no hope of amphibian craft being able to unload this stuff.

Heavy shelling in Cherbourg area, Having a fairly quite time here (Apart from the weather) 100 times better than Sword. 24.00hrs. Enemy aircraft over Utah beach.

June 22nd 1944.

Weather still pretty bad. 3 days at anchor of this beach. No chance of American craft being able to unload this cargo yet. One spark and it's either Heaven or Hell in a matter of seconds. United States Naval Launch alongside, Orders to run our ship onto the beach. Needing the Octane very urgently. We are needing rid of it urgently.

So at 13.10hrs on 22nd June 1944 Ship No 461 weighs anchor and commences a run in on Omaha Beach. By 4pm or ship is high and dry, facing Hitler's Great Atlantic wall.

Needless to say cargo discharge starts immediately, Went ashore, Glad to stretch the legs. Very easy- Pilot ladders over the ships side and we land on beach. Kept to road used by American troops. Many land mines so we didn't need a second telling to keep to the safe road.

Many farms destroyed, still dead cattle lying in the fields. Some families, women and children, are still there in the houses that remain standing. It must have been a nightmare for them.

It's about 6pm so we head for HOME again – our ship on the beach.

Hundreds of German prisoners on beach waiting to embark on U.S. landing craft. A terrible sight. We were told that these men were captured at the Falaise Gap, which was subject to a terrible pounding by American rocket firing Typhoons.

Mostly very young men, about my age and maybe a couple of years younger. Their uniforms in tatters, many badly wounded. Many many stretcher cases.

As seamen we do not see the other side of the war (the war on land) but to me as a civilian it's so sad to see, enemy or not, young men so demoralised. But again, at least for them, their was is over.

Midnight. Still working cargo, American troops continue unloading throughout the night.

No enemy air activity here, although seems to be having a warm time on nearby American Utah beach. Heavy-aircraft fire.

Expect all cargo to be out by morning? Will be glad to see it all out. My nerves have been on edge since we loaded this cargo over a week ago.

June 23rd 1944.

08.00hrs.Lovely morning, Big change in weather. Unloading going well (Non stop). Will complete later today.

16.00hrs. Cargo unloading completed. All American soldiers ashore now. We say goodbye. I am sure, like us, they are glad all this cargo is safely ashore and will help to keep their aircraft flying. 28 hours non-stop unloading is a long spell.

20.00hrs. Ship all ready for sea – but still high and dry on Omaha beach. Hope to be afloat around midnight.

June 24th 1944.

01.00 hrs.All ballast tanks pumped out and commenced heaving out with kedge anchor. Ship moving off beach. All clear and afloat again. Ordered to Capille Roadstead until daylight. Heavy gunfire in distance towards Cherbourg. At anchor.

08.00hrs.Mid-Summers day. Fine clear sky, calm sea (A good to be alive day)

Awaiting our convoy home, (About mid afternoon). Home for me is Clachnaharry, Inverness but at the moment I have to settle for our second home, Southampton.

15.30hrs. Proceeding in convoy, Bound Solent for orders. Not much to shout about this trip, apart from the cargo and the weather. Normandy coast away on the horizon. Convoy at moderate speed. Very warm day, Sunbathing weather but not wearing lifejackets. Longing for a night at home in my own bed with clean sheets and a pair of pyjamas.

Nothing to write about, plodding on. Waves of bombers and Fighters (Ours) passing overhead on their way out. Midnight. Nearing our coast, Convoy slow. – Awaiting daylight.

June 25th 1944.
Passing I.O.W. on way to anchorage. So ends another crossing to the Invasion Beaches. Thank you God for another safe voyage – Proceed to Southampton Docks, sirens sounding, flying bombs over City. Deadly weapons. Sorry for the people ashore. Commenced loading cargo.

June 26th 1944.
08.00 hrs.Cargo loading going well. Very cloudy today. Air raid sirens sounding again. Flying bombs overhead, falling beyond City.
16.00hrs. Heavy rain falling, fierce thunder and lightening storm, but soon clearing.
23.00 hrs. Sirens sounding again. Flying bombs over City …Nasty!

June 27th 1944.
Will finish loading sometime today, weather not so good, not much to say., it's all go.
18.00 hrs. Loaded ready for sea. Proceed to Solent. Join convoy for "You Know Where"
Midnight, Proceeding in convoy, weather bad. Ship in fine trim. Sea moderate in channel. Expected off French coast early afternoon.
12.00 hrs. Normandy coast stretching away ahead of us. Moderate to fresh off shore breeze.
15.30 hrs. Anchored off American beachhead. Omaha. I'm sure the Yanks like us, we seem to be invited over here quite often. Maybe they like our Ships cooks fresh baked bread.
Seems fine and quite on shore so far. American soldiers on board. Commence discharge cargo.

Midnight. Will continue discharge all night. Enemy air-activity much less here, more in Cherbourg area, With air strikes established on shore, we don't have the same amount of visits from the enemy planes.

June 30th 1944.
Fine, clear day. Will finish unloading cargo today. Seven Naval personnel on board for passage home. Men from T.L.C. (Tank Landing Craft) – which will not be returning home.
16.00 hrs. All cargo discharge complete. Proceed to assembly anchorage.
20.00 hrs. Lovely warm evening. No convoy home today. Will have another night at anchor viewing the shoreline. Large formations of Halifax and Liberated Bombers passing over our Ships. German A.A. Guns opening up on them, must be bombing enemy positions. Caen area.
First formation coming out again, that must have been a concentrated raid. They have only been in about ten minutes, passing over us again on their way home. Saw Bomber crash – hope they all come out safely. Heavy beach smoke now rising over the top of the hill.
Midnight. German planes over convoy area. Flares dropping, sky lit up. Coming in again. Shore A.A. guns giving them hell. We are not allowed to open fire. Bombs dropped and they are away.
01.00hrs All quiet.

July 1st 1944.
04.00 hrs. Heavy fighting in progress on- shore. Caen area, These last two hours. Sky alight with gun flashes.
Never thought, as a Sailor, I would be so near a battlefield. Daylight coming. Our sailing time is expected to be 14.00 hrs today.
Sailing once more for England. Going further away from Normandy with every turn of the propeller. Everything OK. Maintaining good speed. Visibility very poor with heavy rain.

A good night for a comfy chair by the fireside.
Midnight. Similar weather conditions. Reduced speed until
dawn.

July 2nd 1944.
AM."BIG NEWS" Trixie the Ships cat and Normandy Heroine
has just given birth to twins. We expected them to be born in
France but she must have decided to wait a little longer for
England. Another 2 have arrived. Total 4. She is a Scottish lady
and they have a Scottish father. She must have slipped ashore in
Leith before we sailed for the South.
Passing Needles I.O.W. on our way in.
07.00 hrs. Ship anchored in Solent again. Thank God for our
safe return. Also the safe delivery of Trixie's bairns. No orders
so far.

July 4th 1944.
Proceed to Southampton Docks and commence loading cargo.
Not much to say. Usual air raid warnings throughout the night.

July 5th 1944.
Noon.Cargo almost completely loaded. May sail tonight.
16.00 hrs. Ship ready for sea. Leave Docks. Proceed to Solent
anchorage.
20.00 Hrs. At anchorage, awaiting further orders to sail.
Midnight. Proceeding slowly in convoy. Destination American
Beach (Omaha) for orders. I know they must love us over there.

July 6th 1944.
04.00 hrs Dawn and every sign of a decent day. Convoy
increased speed to arrive off beaches early evening.
08.00 hrs. Our Bombers/Fighters passing overhead on way out.
French coast on horizon. Heavy gunfire in distance.
Naval escorts dropping depth charges behind convoy. Ship
vibrates with underwater explosions.

18.00 hrs. Arrived off beachhead. Ordered to proceed to the Port of Isigny Sur Mer, near Carenton. Anchored, awaiting French Pilot.

Two French Pilots on board. Proceed up canal to the town of Isigny.

Midnight. Moored along side quay at Isigny. Heavy artillery fire a few miles away. Ordered to lower our Barrage Balloon to mast height. Germans too close here for my liking. Somehow, I seem to be afraid for the first time. I don't know why. Much happier at anchor off the beaches. |Watches maintained here throughout the night. The heavy firing continues all night.

July 7th 1944.

Seems strange to find yourself in a French Port, only one month after D. Day.

Local people down at port possibly looking at the first British Ship in the harbour since pre-war days.

No shore leave here – don't know why. The Ship berthed so close to the town. French flags flying from some buildings.

People seem friendly – Kids having a good time, enjoying slices of bread and jam and chocolate from the crew.

This is a fine day, steady stream on our aircraft crossing the sky. Heavy battle raging a few miles away.

Midday. Cargo discharge going well – Maybe able to leave port at high tide tonight.

18.00 hrs. Still unloading cargo, Unfortunately no hope of leaving here tonight. Heavy fighting seems to be raging a few miles inland – Local people thought Germans had broken through our lines.

We are approx 7 miles from Carenton, A BAD NIGHT.

July 8th 1944.

We will be leaving here in a few hours time. Quite a nice place it seems, they say it is badly damaged by the tide of war.

12.00 hrs. Goodbye to Isigny Sur Mer. French people waving goodbye to us as we make our way out towards the sea.
Homeward bound again, nothing much to say about the passage home.

July 9th 1944.
At anchor in Solent awaiting orders. Our orders are… Proceed to Plymouth – But still in Solent awaiting weather to moderate – Summer time ??

July 10th 1944.
Midday.Weather not moderating – Still at anchor in Solent. Air raid warnings sounding ashore.
Flying bombs passing over Solent at approx 15 minute intervals – Ten of these missiles have passed over so far. Tremendous sound as they plunge to earth. Sorry for the people ashore.

July 11th 1944.
Dawn breaking, proceeding towards Plymouth – Sea now moderate.
16.00 hrs. Anchor in Plymouth Roads. Watches maintained throughout the night.
A SLEEP !! 4 Hrs off, 4 Hrs on – Big Deal.

July 12th 1944.
11.00 hrs.Weigh anchor and proceed to our loading berth in Plymouth Harbour. Maybe a couple of days here and a chance to go ashore for a change.
Plymouth, badly damaged by air raids. Such a beautiful City, lovely people.

July 15th 1944.

08.00 hrs.Prepare to sail, all cargo completely loaded. Ship ready for sea.
09.00 hrs. Outward bound from Plymouth to Normandy. Weather not very good.
I will always remember the summer of 1944 – that was not.
16.00 hrs. heavy fog closing in, visibility much poorer. Convoy reduced speed. Thick fog throughout night. Proceeding slowly in convoy.

July 16th 1944.
Similar weather conditions prevail.
12.00 hrs. Fog lifting a bit, not far from the French coast now. Some of our convoy scattered here and there – beginning to re-group again.
14.00 hrs. Approaching beachhead. Proceeding in shore to anchorage and prepare ship for cargo discharge.
15.00 hrs. Discharge of cargo commenced. Continuous unloading until midnight. Work stopped. Fog closing in. Amphibian Craft cannot operate in this weather. No cargo unloading this night.
A peaceful night in the offing. Dense fog shrouding the beaches. No aircraft to bother us tonight.

July 17th 1944.
Soldiers on board. Unloading resumed, making up for lost time. Very warm today and no let up in the unloading, weather permitting. Another 24 hrs or so will see us unloaded.
23.20 hrs. Hostile planes over. Bombing beaches. Heavy anti-aircraft fire coming from shore. Most merchant ships are not allowed to open fire on aircraft now. Naval and selected ships in anchorage only.

July 18th 1944.

Will finish cargo discharge today. But amphibian craft having a hard time with a heavy swell running in on the beach.

13.00 hrs. All cargo out. Proceed to assembly anchorage to await convoy home.

Tremendous artillery battle raging in the direction of Caen. Seems like a new offensive push is in progress. No orders to sail. Looks like another night here in anchorage.

July 19th 1944.

On our way home. Heavy fog closing in. Convoy proceeding slowly. Visibility almost- zero. This weather continues all night.

July 20th 1944.

Midday.Approaching Plymouth sound, no orders so far. Anchored off Plymouth, A quiet night.

July 21st 1944.

Not wanted here. Ordered to proceed to Poole, Dorset. On our way, weather conditions poor, moderate sea, sky overcast.

18.00 hrs. Still plodding on, nothing much to say. Expect to arrive off Poole early am on 22nd July.

09.00 hrs. Off Poole harbour. Not wanted in post meantime. No berth available. Must anchor off Port until Sunday.

12.00 hrs. Anchored off Port until sometime Sunday. Weather good.

July 23rd 1944.

Lovely bright summers day, a very changeable summer, weather wise. Looks very peaceful on shore.

11.00 hrs. Weight anchor. Proceed toward Poole harbour and loading berth. Hope for at least a couple of days here.

Met ward of S.S. KAIDA, had a few words, maintains we will be lucky if we enjoy a glass of beer here. Poole is almost DRY. Not to worry. A bar is the least of our worries.

July 24th 1944.

24 hrs in Port, non- stop loading. A miserable few hours ashore. Unable to phone home. Poole harbour is beautiful, maybe after the war I will have more time to see this beautiful place.

15.00 hrs. All ready for sea again.

18.00 hrs. Proceed to anchorage again and await orders to sail. This will be our 6th voyage to Normandy.

Midnight. A peaceful night. Watches as usual maintained.

July 25th 1944.

04.00 hrs.Joined convoy off Poole Roads, Bound British Sector Arromanches. Fast convoy, will be off Arromanches early evening.

17.00 hrs. Arrived at Arromanches, what a change, it s almost a month since we were last here.

Now we have the Mulberry Harbour – man made. No more off-loading into amphibian craft off the beaches.

20.00 hrs. Soldiers start unloading only 2 hrs after our arrival here. They tell us that George Formby and Co are giving the troops a show in Arromanches – Not for us as we are not allowed shore leave. Ship must remain on constant standby.

23.00 hrs. Enemy planes over Arromanches. All hell let loose, terrific barrage going up. Raids continue until early hours of morning, Continue discharge all night.

July 26th 1944.

Dawn.We hope to complete discharge today pm.

14.30 hrs. All cargo discharged, great credit to the soldiers who worked non-stop around the clock, uncaring about the enemy activity, as long as the vital supplies are unloaded. To anchor as usual. Can see the coastal Tanker, Ben Robinson, close by (A Ship I know).

15.30 hrs. At anchor until daylight. Probably a grandstand view of any Fireworks tonight.

23.40 hrs. German planes over beachhead, getting a hot reception. – Why don't they give up. Flare dropping – Place all lit up. Bombs dropping, many planes over. Red glow in sky, fires seen in distance – Heavy A.A. fire from shore.

July 27th 1944.
02.00 hrs. They are back again. Tremendous barrage from our A.A. guns ashore. We are not allowed to open fire on aircraft. During and shortly after the landings there was a lot of indiscriminate firing from Merchant Ships. Possibly- Some of our own fighters were at risk.
04.00 hrs. All quiet again.
Cargo will be completely unloaded this morning.
11.00 hrs. Joined escorts and proceeding home. Weather not so good, winds increasing. Sea moderate to rough.
16.00 hrs. My get to anchorage in Solent before dark.
23.05 hrs. Passed examination Ship and through harbour boom to anchorage.
Midnight + 30.
At anchor, night watches – as usual.
So ends our 6th voyage to Normandy. One month and twenty days since D.Day.
I thank you God for looking after us.

July 28th 1944.
AM. Still at anchor in Solent. Expect to enter Southampton Docks to load again sometime today.
11.00 hrs. Our Bombers passing over Solent on their way across.

July 29th 1944.
Leave anchorage. Proceed towards Southampton Docks to load.

August 1st 1944.
Leaving our "Home Port" (adopted) after 3 days in harbour. Ship fully loaded and proceed (as usual) to anchor in Solent to await convoy (as usual). Weather fairly good (Not usual) with fresh/strong N.E. wind.

August 2nd 1944.

04.00 hrs (Dawn).Sailed from Solent on our way again. Sky clear, fresh north/easterly winds. Proceed towards Normandy. Not sure of our destination yet.

17.00 hrs. Arrive off Gold Beach for Port En Bessin. Awaiting tide and French Harbour Pilot.

Pilot on board. Proceeding in.

22.30 hrs. Moored in harbour.

August 3rd 1944.

Cargo unloading, working throughout and with no delays we may be able to leave here at high tide tonight.

We will leave Port En Bessin tonight. Hope before the night flyers pay us their usual visits.

22.00 hrs. Discharge almost complete, prepare ship for sea. Pilot on board. Cleared Port and proceed to assembly anchorage.

A.A. guns in action ashore. We will remain at anchor until AM Friday.

August 4th 1944.

Fine clear day. On our way home.

Allied Bombers-Fighters passing over convoy on their way to French coast.

22.30 hrs. Anchored inside boom. Defence vessels in Solent. Nothing very exciting to report. Good passage home. So ends our 7th voyage to Normandy. We will have to stay at anchor here for a few days. Then into Southampton Docks to load.

August 10th 1944.

Vessel completed loaded once more. Leave docks for anchorage. Quiet time in Southampton. Not so many V1 or V2s this time. Maybe they are being SORTED OUT in the Pas De Calais area.

August 11th 1944.

02.00 hrs.Proceed in convoy. With smaller convoys these days we seem to maintain maximum speed, we have good Naval escorts and as the war in Europe progresses we are not bothered too much with attacks on convoys.

It is now 2 months and 5 days since the landings.

16.00 hrs. Approaching Gold beach. Orders from Examination vessel to proceed towards Port En Bessin. French pilot on board.

19.30 hrs. Vessel moored alongside. No doubt we will have the usual visit tonight from the odd German plane or two having a go. The A.A. ashore is now tremendous between the two beachheads of Gold and the American Omaha. So the Hun gets a hot reception.

August 12th 1944.

Dawn. Commencing unloading- an early start and it will continue until completion.

Port En Bissen is a tidal port and naturally ships can only enter and leave at certain state of tide.

18.00 hrs. Still unloading, maybe complete by midnight.

August 13th 1944.

04.00 hrs. Daylight, now cargo completely discharged, leaving Port En Bissen. A fine summers day and very peaceful.

10.00 hrs. Convoy leaves for home. – Solent.

21.15 hrs. At anchor. A very uneventful crossing (ten hours) . As a matter of fact nothing very important to write about. This day, 13th August ends our eight crossing to Normandy. My unofficial diary seems to be getting very repetitive. Depart – Arrive. Arrive – Depart. Still, we are a happy crew and have been together in this small ship, in very confined quarters since leaving Leith in April. Maybe soon we will be suspended from our Normandy duties – maybe.

15th August 1944.

06.00 hrs. After two days at anchor, it's proceed to Southampton Docks to load.

07.00 hrs. Moored alongside and commenced loading IMMEDIATELY.

19.00 hrs. Cargo completed. 12 hrs non stop. Leaving docks.

21.00 hrs. Anchored awaiting sailing orders.
After only 24 hrs completely loaded and waiting to sail.

August 16th 1944.
On our way across again. A very fast turnaround (Good old
Southampton Dockers) They must be fed up with the sight of us
and a fast crossing, it you can call 10 knots fast !
Port En Bessin again. They must like us here. No doubt when
darkness comes in we shall have our usual visitors.
23.00 hrs. Moored in harbour.

August 17th 1944.
Cargo going well. Hope to leave here tonight/later tonight.
22.00 hrs. Pilot on board, leaving for anchorage.
Heavy artillery firing well inland and continuous all through the
night. Port En Bessin lies between the British and American
lines.

August 18th 1944.
On our way home, Passing through a lot of floating wreckage.
Weather very good.
21.30hrs. Arrived in Solent and ship at anchor. Watches
maintained 4hrs on 4hrs off. It's hardly worth turning in.
Longing for a long hot bath, a clean pair of pyjamas – What are
pyjamas ?. Some nice new clean clothes and a fine long sleep in
my bed at home. Voyage No9 to Normandy safely completed.

August 19th 1944.
Southampton Docks to load. Awaiting cargo – maybe a few
days in port this time.

August 24th 1944.
Cargo completed and out to anchorage. 5 days wait this time.
Unusual to be in port for so long.

August 26th 1944.

On passage to Sword Beach. Heavy fog banks hanging over the sea, reduced speed.

15.00hrs. Closing examination ship off Sword Beach for orders. Ordered to anchor.

20.00 hrs. Still at anchor, weather very unsettled.

August 27th 1944.

Fine warm summer morning. Everywhere peaceful and quiet. No orders yet, no enemy planes near beaches.

August 28th 1944.

Proceeding towards Arromanches (Mulberry Harbour). No air activity here – no activity of any kind. Cargo going well – No shore leave, Still we had a couple of days break in Southampton. Unloading non-stop. Now complete.

August 29th 1944.

14.00 hrs. On our way out to anchorage to await orders.

August 30th 1944.

A very quiet time, well on our way home. Moderate sea making good time.

22.00 hrs. We are at anchor in Solent. A very quiet uneventful time. Things are getting better, at least for us on the Beachheads. This ends our 10th crossing to Normandy.

August 31st 1944.

Proceeding towards Southampton Docks to load. Loading commenced IMMEDIATELY and will continue until completed.

September 1st 1944.

17.00 hrs. All cargo completed. Preparing ship for sea. Anchored and await convoy escort, destination CAEN.

September 2nd 1944.

04.00 hrs Dawn breaking, on our way. Blowing a gale, ship labouring, mod to heavy sea.

10.00 hrs. Winds reaching 60. Ship rolling heavily, fear for cargo, not making much headway. Ship turned round and heading back towards English Coast.

22.15 hrs. Ship anchored in lea of the land. Sea watches throughout the night. Life gets tedious.

September 3rd 1944.

AM. Making another attempt. Wind and sea moderating, making fairly good headway.

23.30 hrs. Anchored off entrance to Caen Canal, Ouistreham, Awaiting daylight.

September 4th 1944.

Proceed to lock gates up Caen Canal. Ouistreham in ruins. I am certainly not surprised, having laid offshore and watched that area taking tremendous poundings night and day. Some French people wave to us from canal banks. Many of our Airborne regiment Gliders strewn along the banks where they landed – possibly D.Day minus 1. We have passed four bridges and are now approaching the ruined City of Caen.

We are the first British Ship carrying ordinance cargo to enter this Port sine it was liberated. The docks are in fair condition, but the town is a sorry sight to see. Our French Pilot says that about three thousand French people are buried beneath the ruins. I have never smelled death before. But believe me, this ruined town smells of death – The town our soldiers fought so hard for during the first 2 months of the Landings. Nothing but a shell.

September 5th 1944.

PM. Cargo completely discharged. A quick turn around. We leave Caen now. A place where I don't think I shall ever forget.

On our way through the canal again towards Ouistreham and out to sea. Raining heavily today.

Anchored to await our sailing orders.

Le Harve is burning. Heavy explosions and fire over town.

Enemy bombers passing high over beaches.

September 6th 1944.

Midday. Three months have passed since D.Day and we are still here.

On our way home. Will reach anchorage at Solent before dark.

21.00 hrs. Examination Vessel orders to anchor for night.

September 7th 1944.

Still awaiting orders.

This ending our 11th voyage to Normandy.

16.00 hrs. Proceed towards Southampton Docks.

18.00 hrs. Moored alongside to commence loading.

September 8th 1944.

19.00 hrs. Completely loaded and ready for sea. Did not get long here this time. 24 hrs.

21.00 hrs. At anchor. Awaiting orders to sail.

September 9th 1944.

06.00 hrs. On our way to Arromanches. Arrive sometime this evening. We are Commodore Vessel (Merchant Ship in lead of convoy). First time.

20.00 hrs. Arrived at Arromanches (Mulberry Harbour). Commenced unloading immediately.

September 10th 1944.

Unloading all day also Monday and Tuesday. No problems here. No hostile activity of any kind. The Mulberry Harbour – pre-Fabricated in England and floated across the channel to Sword Beach area and finally in place off Gold Beach, Arromanches.

September 12th 1944.
Daylight. Sailed immediately – A straight run home – an easy passage.
Midnight. At anchor in Solent. Thus ending our 12th voyage to Normandy. Life at sea is much more civilised lately.

September 13th 1944.
Loading once more in Southampton. A quiet day, continuous loading until cargo complete. Expect to finish cargo tomorrow evening.

September 14th 1944.
08.00 hrs. Cargo completely loaded. Leaving Port tonight for anchorage.

September 15th 1944.
05.00 hrs Outward bound to Arromanches. Weather fine and clear, expect about 10-11 hours crossing. Good weather.
15.00 hrs. We are in sight of Normandy coast.
18.00 hrs. Moored alongside Mulberry Harbour and discharge of cargo commences immediately.

September 16th 1944.
Allowed ashore here for the first time. Went into small town of Bayeux today. A lovely town, hardly touched by tide of war. Women very smart and well dressed- to me after 3 months of this all women look smart and pretty. Cafes are open but we have no French Francs to buy a beer. I don't think they would handle a Scotch £1.00 note.

September 17th 1944.
07.00 hrs. Ship ready for sea. Proceeding home for Southampton.
19.00 hrs. Had a good crossing. Home in good time. Approx 12 hrs. Anchor until daylight in Solent. So ends our 13th voyage with war material to Normandy. 13. Lucky for us, Sorry to say not for many of our comrades.

September 19th 1944.
Received orders to proceed to London. Looks like goodbye to
Normandy. Three months and 13 days since D.Day.
On passage to River Thames for orders. Fine clear weather.
Passing through Straits of Dover, rumbles of gunfire far away
on the French coast.

September 20th 1944.
17.00 hrs We are at anchor in Thames off Gravesend. Maybe
now its home for a few days leave. Maybe. I do hope so. Four
years of war at sea with little or no leave.

September 21st 1944.
Proceeding towards Tilbury Docks to load. Cargo for Ostende,
Belgium. The first Belgian Port to be opened for shipping. The
war progresses.
Ostende – Tilbury and possibly so on until the end of the war in
Europe.

I end my secret diary of the Normandy Operations.
If I died my diary would have died with me.
As a civilian Seaman in the Merchant Service to me it was a
great honour and privilege to be involved in such a great
campaign. To serve beside the great British Warships off the
Normandy Beaches.
The HMS RENOUN, HMS NELSON, HMS WARSPITE &
HMS RAMILLIES. THE HEAVY BOYS - and to be
associated with the British Soldiers on Sword, Gold and Juno
Beaches, also the many American friends on Omaha and Utah.
I will always remember the kindness of the people of Wapping,
E. London, as we waited in London Docks before sailing to the
South coast. The Dock workers in Southampton, Plymouth and
Poole who kept us on the move.
Not forgetting the faithful little ship No. 461 S.S. HOLBOURN
HEAD of LEITH.

Our Captain, Peter Stickle of Unst – Shetland. A fine example of a Merchant Navy Skipper.
Also my friend, 1st officer George Bain from Wick, Caithness and all the rest of the crew of such a happy ship.
I remained with the Holbourn Head until V.E. Day when we were eventually de-commissioned in Hull.
I had some leave at home in Inverness before resuming my career at sea.

ALBERT.W. BIRD. (Able Seaman)
S.S. HOLBURN HEAD.

Albert Bird and his wife, Betty, on a lifeboat in Aberdeen

ARTHUR GREIG

Arthur is one of those great characters who are worthy of mention and could write a book on his life experiences. I have one story told to me by Arthur's kindred spirit Sandy Philips. During The Second World War Arthur was captured by the Japanese and put in a Prison of War Camp. Towards the end of the War the Americans arrived and Arthur and his fellow prisoners were rescued from the starvation and disease which they had to endure in the camp. The Americans took Arthur out of the camp and he was put on a ship with his fellow prisoners to be taken to Japan. The ship was torpedoed and sunk by the Americans. Of the 1700 on board the ship only 600 survived, including Arthur, who spent 20 hours in the shark infested waters clinging to debris. Eventually they were rescued by another ship but unfortunately it was a Japanese ship which took Arthur and his comrades back to a prison of war camp.

When the war ended Arthur was put on an American plane and as he was being flown to freedom it got into difficulties and Arthur had to put on a parachute and jump out of the plane as it tumbled to the sea. This was the first time Arthur had used a parachute but it saved his life. He told my brother that his main concern was that the packet of cigarettes he had been given by the Americans were going to get wet and would be ruined. Arthur landed safely in the sea and had to spend another twenty hours in the sea until he was rescued by a New Zealand destroyer and taken to Dunedin.

Arthur survived the War but had suffered great cruelty at the hands of the Japanese by starvation and disease and I am sure that Arthur's wife Meg would regret sending Arthur to the shop for messages as often as not Arthur would return with two of the items he had been sent for. I am sure Arthur would have made sure that the larder was always full. It must be one of the worst forms of torture to deprive your fellow man from food.

Sadly as I write this story Arthur has passed away; it was on 24th December 2004 and I regret that this is the only story I have of this great character.

The Greig family ran a bus company in Inverness. The Depot was on Telford Street and is now the car-park for the Co-op Supermarket. Arthur's son Andrew is still resident in Inverness and lives with his partner in the Dalneigh area of Inverness.

HOGMANAY

At the beginning of the twentieth century Christmas was not celebrated in Scotland, the main celebration was the New Year. The women of the household would have all the food prepared on Hogmanay ready for New Years Day. In many parts of Scotland a large steak pie would be prepared for New Years Day Dinner and scotch broth was popular.

Our friend Karen Mackay told us that in the Shetlands a traditional soup served at the New Year was made from salted mutton and turnip. The mutton was called Rysted Mutton. This was mutton that had been salted to preserve it and it had to be soaked in water several times before it could be used.

On Hogmanay the whole of the house had to be cleaned and dusted. The belief was that if the house was not clean on New Years day it would not be clean for the rest of the year. Also food and drink were put on the table ready for the New Year.

After the Second World War Whisky was expensive and I can remember that my grandfather Albert Gibson was allowed one bottle of whisky for the New Years celebration. My Aunt Isobel Gibson sent the smallest glasses she could find home from Canada to my grandfather to try and make his bottle go further. Today large tumblers of whisky are poured and the uisge-beatha (the water of life) flows more freely.

In the 1950s and '60s it was common for most of the community to leave their doors unlocked after The Bells (Midnight) to welcome their First Foot of the New Year.

The first foot was preferably tall, dark and handsome. This was thought to bring good luck for the rest of the New Year. I can remember my mother taking no chances and before The Bells someone with some of the required good looks and dark hair would go out the backdoor of our house and enter at the front door to be welcomed as the First Foot after the Bells. I have heard it said that coal could by its black colour allow someone with lighter hair to First Foot a household.
The First Foot would have his bottle of whisky and when he entered the house would offer everyone a dram from his bottle and when this was finished a dram was returned from the bottle in the house. The First Foot would take a piece of coal into the house and this would be put on the fire. He would have some shortbread or some other food when he entered the house and would give this to the woman of the house and she would put it on the table. The tradition was that if food and drink and fuel entered the house on New Years Day they would remain for the rest of the year. We may find these superstitions a bit stupid but

these traditions go back to a time when hunger and disease could wipe out whole communities.

The Hogmany party could last well into the next day and some large hangovers would be suffered on New Years Day. Of course someone could be given a Joram (Gaelic Word). This was the same as a hair of the dog that bit you to try and relieve your suffering.

A guest leaving the company in the early hours of the morning could be offered "A wee Deoch and Dorius" which was a parting drink as the guest left the household.

In many parts of Scotland up until the latter part of the Twentieth Century the Auld New Year was celebrated. This is on the twelfth of January and was the date of New Years Day on a previous calendar.

From the 25th December until the 12th January there is an hour of extra daylight in the north of Scotland. This was a good reason to celebrate the New Year especially in farming communities who could make good use of this early daylight. Also in the countryside a shotgun would be fired to herald in the New Year and to chase away any evil spirits. If you go outside in the Highlands after The Bells you may still hear the gun go off along with the fireworks on a New Years morning. After the dinner on New Years Day many people would visit friends and relatives and another party might begin.

My memories of the 1950s is of the black and white television and watching Andy Stewart and his Highland Dancers and of Findlay Macrae reciting "A Wee Cock Sparra".

Nowadays Christmas celebrations have overtaken New Year in Scotland but it is nice to celebrate the old traditions: if we do not they will disappear. The New Years dinner at Elgol, Clachnaharry, would often consist of a haunch of venison given to the family by Bob Cameron, a family friend who was a gamekeeper and worked for an estate at Mullardoch which is above Cannich in the Highlands. This would be roasted and served with vegetables. We would start with broth made with vegetables and maybe a piece of mutton. Bob would sometimes take us children in his Commer van along to the Clach Pub and he would buy us crisps and lemonade and we would sit in the back of the van as Bob would entertain those in the pub by singing and playing tunes on his moothy (mouth-organ).

Bob Cameron and my grandfather Albert Gibson share a joke as my granny Ann Gibson serves the tea in the front room of Elgol, Clachnaharry. Sadly Bob passed away about two years ago. The tune 'Come By The Hills' was played at Bob's funeral as it was at my brother Watty's Funeral.

DIXONS

I worked for Dixons the printers during the 1960s; they printed mostly postcards. The building was until recently used by the Stratton Dairy and has recently been demolished and replaced by a store selling golf equipment beside the Longman Road Roundabout. I can only describe the factory as a sweat shop and modern Health And Safety Regulations were in their infancy.

The printing machines were in banks of three with one man on each machine for the three primary colours, red, yellow and blue. The noise was unbelievable as the compression rollers for about twenty printing machines came together to impress the image from the printing plate onto the paper sheets and it took some time to get used to the noise and make out what anyone was saying.

We started at 8 o'clock am and I knew I was about to be late if I heard the hooter going off at the Rose Street foundry as I cycled along Rose Street. We had an hour for lunch at one o'clock and worked from two until five. The machines had to be printing for the maximum time and we had to print several thousand impressions to qualify for a very small bonus.

When I had completed what was supposed to be an apprenticeship of about five years I left this job and went to work in England. When I was interviewed for the job I was asked what chemicals we used for the printing presses at Dixons. When I told them one of the solvents used was xylene they told me that this chemical was banned in England as it was thought to cause cancer.

The solvent was used to mix with the ink for the printing presses. I believe this is now called a Control Substance and should have been used with great care if at all. In Dixons we used it for cleaning machines and the floor and we had a bucket of at the side of the machine and would wash our hands and arms in it to remove ink splatters. There would be people with either yellow or red or blue hands depending on which machine they were working on.

On Friday afternoon the machines were stopped at three o'clock for cleaning. I would sometimes be given two machines to clean and by stopping time I would be staggering about with the effects from the solvent fumes. The old hands would head for the pub and after the effects of the solvent fumes would be quite drunk after a couple of pints of beer. I suppose we were the equivalent of modern solvent abusers but to us it was all part of a day's work. Such is ignorance.

GORDON MILLER

Gordon was another apprentice about the same age as myself. In the mornings Gordon and I would go over to the bakers beside Dixon's with a list of the orders for pies and buns for the journeymen who had to stay beside their machines. We would do half the journeymen each and Gordon had gone ahead of me to the bakers. As I was about to enter the bake house, I saw there was a large tray of shortbread at the entrance of the bake house, placed on the floor to cool. The unusual thing about this tray of shortbread was that it had the footprint of Gordon's size eleven shoe stamped on it. Gordon had walked over it and had not even noticed. Gordon always seemed in a bit of a dream world, maybe it was the fumes. Sadly Gordon died young, in his twenties.

THE STRATH

The Strath was the Strathpeffer Pavilion and in the 1960s it was used as a Dance Hall. I remember reading that, in their early days, The Beatles were booked to play at the Strath when they were in the Highlands, but it did not happen.

A bus would leave Farraline Park in Inverness on a Friday night stopping at Beauly, Muir of Ord and Dingwall on the way. This was usually a double decker bus on what is still known as The Great North Road and was at one time the only road to the North and West. At the entrance to the bus at the rear there was a steel pole and as the bus sped along the road any male who had been drinking beer before getting on the bus could relieve himself onto the road holding onto this pole. There was no door - it was an open entrance at the rear.

My old pal The Driver (Lindsay Redford) told me that he and his friends took great delight in trying to give the bus driver a heart attack by waiting until the bus was going round a tight bend in the road then throwing their weight to one side of the rear. A Strath bus driver's lot was not always a happy one. Because of the trouble on the bus a police escort had to be arranged.

At the Dance we would often have touring Irish Show Bands who could play all types of music including the latest hits. They were quite superb. Towards the end of the night I remember a fight broke out between two women. A large ring of dancers encircled the pair as they tried to scratch each other and pull lumps of hair out and rolling about on the floor. The Band would shout "Fight, Fight!" to attract the Bouncers who eventually arrived and broke the fight up.

After a Friday night out, that was about the end of the money and Saturday would be spent sipping a pint of beer in a pub in the town centre, trying to make it last, and playing darts for a pint. Some of the Pubs were The Ordnance Bar, The Black Bull, The Crit, The Drum, The Carlton, The Muirtown Motel and The Hay Loft to name but a few.

RAIGMORE HOSPITAL

I was in Raigmore Hospital in the 1960s. At that time most of the hospital was made up of Nissen Huts. I remember I had a cracked pelvis caused by doing something stupid playing football with a can at the front of Blackpark Filling Station where I worked in the evenings part time. I also had a job working at Dixons Postcard factory in the Longman where I was serving an apprenticeship.

A work-mate from Dixons came to visit me in hospital and he had a present for me from the work force. This was a packet of cigarettes in a flat box. They were Bristol Tipped and there were 25 cigarettes in the box. This may not seem unusual but at this time I was sixteen years old.

I was confined to bed. I had a traction device on my leg which kept me in the same position and a weight attached to my leg went over the end of the bed. I had to stay in this position for some weeks until my pelvis had healed. In the next bed to me was a man who worked in the construction industry at Aultbea in Wester

Ross. He had his jaw wired up as it had been broken. He said he had been in a brawl and had been hit with a truncheon by a policeman who was trying to quieten him down. He was recovering from the effect of the anaesthetic after the operation and tried to sit up in bed. He asked me if I had a cigarette and I gave him one of the Bristol Tipped I had been given. He smoked part of the cigarette and as he was still quite weak after the operation he could not finish it. As there was no ashtray on his bedside cabinet he reached up and stubbed it out on the top.

This may seem hard to believe today when cigarettes are banned in hospitals but in the 1960s I remember patients smoking in the wards and smoking in bed. If the smoke became too much for the other patients a window was opened to allow the air to clear.

When I was a teenager a cigarette would be partly smoked and stubbed out about half way through. The remainder was called a Tabby and was kept behind the ear or in the top pocket of your jacket until you wanted to smoke it.

THE INVERNESS HIGH SCHOOL 1960

At the shop which still stands on Montague Row we would call in at lunch times and would be sold a fag and a match. Cigarettes could be bought in packets of five but, as I said, one cigarette could be bought. Brands were Woodbine, Capstain and Capstain Full Strength which would blow your head off, Bristol Tipped and Players, Craven A and American cigarettes in soft packages as seen in the movies. Not that we could afford them. Also Menthol tipped cigarettes which tasted like smoking a packet of polo mints.

HIGH SCHOOL DINNERS

I hated school dinners in the High School. Once a week we would have to queue at one of the classrooms for free dinner tickets which were for those children whose parents could not afford to pay for them. Dinner tickets were of different colours and I was conscious of the different colour of my tickets as I handed them over for my dinner. I would try and get enough money to buy a bag of broken biscuits from Woolies on the High Street rather than queue for a free dinner at school.

One day as I was eating my school dinner another pupil opposite me was eating rice pudding and prunes. I could not help noticing that he was eating the stones from the prunes and did not leave the stones at the side of his plate as I did. I asked him if he always ate the stones and he said that he did. I don't know how his digestion system stood up to this or how the lavatory pan which he used stood up to it.

THE BELT

I cannot leave this period of my schooling at the Inverness High School without mentioning the belt.

I have been belted many times and for those who thankfully have never seen it this is how it went. The teacher would take the pupil out to the front of the class and would open the drawer in the teacher's desk and take out the belt. One hand was put on top of the other and held out for the punishment. Three strokes of the belt were normal.

The effect of the belt on the pupil depended on the teacher. A female teacher who did not believe in this form of punishment would have a belt which was supple and soft and would not leave much of a mark on the hands and wrists. But if you pulled your hands back as the belt was about to make contact with your hands causing the belt to hit the teacher on the leg then you knew that the following strokes would be delivered with added venom. Some of the male teachers took a sadistic pleasure in causing large wealds to appear on the hands and wrists of those they were punishing. Also the belts they used were new and hard so as to deliver the maximum amount of damage. I spoke to a Sparky at the Oil Yard at Nigg who showed me a scar which ran up his wrist and his forearm. This was caused by a teacher in the High School belting him. He showed his father the damage done by this teacher and his father told him that he probably deserved it.

I appreciate the difficulty teachers have trying to control unruly youngsters but I don't think the belt was the answer and it is right that this practice was abolished.

THE OIL

I started working at Mcdermott's Oil yard at Ardersier in 1973. This was an eye opener for a young man in his early twenties
I managed to get a job as helper (labourer); the hourly rate was about 50p an hour.
I would work on the yard in an area known as the Pile Rack. This was an area where long lengths of pipe would be welded together. One day I was wandering about this area when an American came along. I would know that he was a High Heid Yin by the colour of his hard hat which was Gold. This was the colour of the hats of the managers. Hard hats were of different colours; red was for welders' blue was for fitters, white was for supervisors or instructors or toilet cleaners. The colour coding would cause some problems for me. The American came towards me and as I was doing nothing at the time I jumped and picked up a gas bottle and made out I was working. I pulled the bottle over the metal rails of the Pile Rack which were about four feet off the ground. The American must have been

suitably impressed as he asked my name and told me to go to the welders' training school the following morning and to tell them that he had sent me.

The next day at the start of the shift I went to the training school and told them I had been told to report there by the American. The instructors were confused as they had a list to work from and my name was not on it. When I told them the name of the American who had sent me they told me to stand at the entrance of the building and went off to try and decide what to do as the American was obviously a senior member in the company. So I stood at the entrance to this building all morning until the hooter went at lunchtime.

There was a chip van that came to the yard at lunchtime and I got some chips to eat and I would go for tea when I saw other workers stopping for a break. When the hooter went at the end of the shift i would go home. This continued until the third day when one of the Instructors took me to the Welders Testing Shed. He took my red hard hat and gave it to the GO (general operative) which was a posh name for someone who cleaned toilets and worked in the canteens. He gave me the white hat worn by the GO and told him to report to another part of the yard.

I now had a job helping the trainee welders as they set up their test pipes in the cubicles in the test shed. The welder had to weld two short pieces of 10 inch pipes together for their test and I would help them set the pipe at an angle of 45 degrees on a stand. I would also keep the welding rod oven full of welding rods, which were used in the test. The welding oven was about three feet square and had heating elements inside to dry the welding rods before they could be used. The rods had to be dried because if they were used when they were damp this could cause the weld to crack.

Another problem was caused by the misuse of the rod oven. It was used by the welders and the instructors to heat pies and sausage rolls for the tea break. This was OK until Les Miller a trainee welder decided to heat a tin of beans in the oven. He did not puncture the top of the tin and as the temperature inside the tin increased it exploded and coated the welding rods with beans and tomato sauce. Les was not very popular with the instructors and spent some considerable time cleaning up the mess and restocking the oven.

As I watched the trainee welders work I would hold a welding mask lens up to my eyes and see what they were doing. A welding inspector would come round and if a weld was not satisfactory the welder would be stopped with the pipe joint only half welded. The welder would go away and would be re-tested on another day. When it was quiet I would put on a welding mask and practice on the part-welded pipe before I removed the pipe from the stand. I worked in the test shed for several weeks until my name came up on the list to go into the welder training school. This was just as well as I was causing some confusion in the welders' testing shed. I was being asked to give my opinion on the welding efforts of trainee welders who thought I was a welding instructor. This was because the toilet cleaner and the Instructor both wore white hard hats.

Because I had learned something about welding as I waited to go into the training school I progressed quite quickly and had soon passed my welding test and was put out onto the Yard to progress under the instruction of American welders who came over to Scotland to teach us. The training course lasted for six weeks and was a very advanced form of training as at this time a welder would have to have spent five years as an apprentice. The trainee welders were called six week wonders. I would continue to learn different welding skills and worked on this yard for over fourteen years. I was at that time in my early twenties and it was quite an eye opener to work with men from all parts of the U.K. and from all over the world.

THE HEY JIMMIES

The Glasgow sub-contractors who worked on the yard were known as the Hey Jimmies. They were squads of Fitters and Fabricators of about twenty men sub-contracted to work alongside the permanent workforce.

In the early days at Ardersier there was a camp on the yard and U.K. and American workers would live in cabins as there was no accommodation available locally due to the large number of men at the yard. At one time there were between two and three thousand people employed at this yard. To get back to the Hey Jimmies: one day I was working alongside an American Instructor called Rab and he said it was difficult to get much sleep at the camp as most nights, and especially at the week-ends, the Glasgow sub-contractors would arrive back at the camp late at night with their cairy-oot and all he would hear was Hey Jimmy this and Hey Jimmy that. To the Glasgow sub-contractor every one was called Jimmy. I think that this American started this name because for years after this all Glasgow sub-contractors were known as Hey-Jimmies. This is not meant to be insulting to the people of Glasgow who I enjoyed working with and who have a marvelous sense of humour.

THE BRANDED HICKY

I believe that a Hicky is the modern name for what in my day was known as a love bite, a mark left on the neck which was a dead give-away that some sort of romantic liaison had taken place. One young sub-contractor was due to go home to Glasgow after working for three weeks at the oil yard at Ardersier. They got one weekend off in four weeks. On the Thursday he was getting very concerned as the Hicky showed no sign of going away and his wife would spot it. His work-mates were sympathetic and got together to try and find a solution to the problem.

The next day was Friday and a solution was found. Three of the young man's work-mates got a hold of him and held him on the ground and another work-mate had a heated welding rod ready and branded the Hicky. So after some struggling and squealing the problem was solved and the young man could go home to his wife and his marriage would be safe. His wife would probably feel sorry for him with that nasty burn he had on his neck from an accident at work. Wasn't he fortunate to have such helpful work-mates? I do like a happy ending.

THE WILDER-BEAST

Jimmy's work-mates named him the Wilder-beast. Jimmy was a welder and was known to roam great distances from his place of work at Ardersier Oil Yard. I remember my friend Woody, who was a sub-contracted welding foreman, talking to me about Jimmy and he said he was going to 'letter' Jimmy for being absent from his place of work for such a long time. (A 'letter' was a disciplinary warning letter.)

I was a Welding Foreman but I was employed by Macdermotts who owned the Yard. I told Woody he couldn't do that as Jimmy was a friend of the Driver's (Lindsay Redford) who was our main form of entertainment at the lunch breaks with his stories of life in the bothy and how big a batch (meal) he could make in his eighteen inch frying pan. And I would say to Woody, 'Anyway don't you know what time of the year it is? Wilder-beasts can roam for miles in the summer months'. Woody would go away shaking his head unable to understand the strange people he was working alongside.

KEITHSON

Keith was a General Foreman who was in charge of other foremen and their men. He was a Geordie and had the habit of calling everyone Son and so he was known as Keithson. He was friendly with my friend Woody and when he was paid of from the oil industry he bought a fish and chip shop in Kyle of Lochalsh on the West coast of Scotland. About twenty years later as Keithson was working at Kyle he was speaking to someone who told him that his old friend Woody was seriously ill. Keithson told this person that he was very sorry to hear this and took out his wallet and produced a twenty pound note and told the person to give the note to Woody as he was probably in financial difficulty. But as he was about to part with the note he changed his mind and told the person 'On second thoughts I won't do that Son as Woody would only be offended', and put the note back in his wallet.

LESTER

Lester was the nickname of Les Miller. I will call him Les in this story. Les worked as a welder at the Oil Yard at Ardersier in the 1970s. Les and Stan Williamson, another welder, were part of a syndicate and won money in a competition called *Spot the Ball* which was run by one of the newspapers. Les decided to buy a new car with his winnings and chose a BMC MG Midget sports car. Les had no end of trouble with his new car and was always back and fore to the garage complaining about faults he had found. Some of the faults would have been genuine as the British motor industry did not have a very good reputation for quality at this time.

When Les was at work he had his lunch in the canteen along with the hundreds of other men who worked on the yard. The canteen had internal telephones linked to other parts of the yard. One day, a phone rang in the canteen and someone answered it. They shouted to Les and said it was a call for him. Les answered and was surprised to find that the call was from Lord Stokes the Managing Director of the motor company BMC. (It was from Richy Burnside another welder on an internal line.) Lord Stokes told Les that he was sorry to hear about the trouble he was having with his new car and told him to go to the BMC garage in Inverness, which was Macrae and Dicks, and he would find a new car to replace the one he was having so much trouble with.

When Les heard this he left the canteen and went to his supervisor to get his clock card so he could leave the yard and head to Inverness to pick up his new car. Of course when Les arrived at the garage he found that nobody knew what he was talking about and knew nothing about a new car courtesy of Lord Stokes. Les finally realized that he had been done and headed back to work. After this episode if anyone mentioned the name of Richy Burnside to Les he would mutter something like 'That B------ '

Les passed away recently after a long illness and I am sure there will be others like myself who will miss him; he was one of those characters who cannot be replaced.

WULLIE AND THE SHOVEL

Wullie was a Fitting Foreman and had a squad of men working for him at the Ardersier Yard. Wullie had to sign chits of paper so his men could get tools etc out of the Tool Store. One day, Wullie needed a shovel out of the store and wrote out a chit and sent one of his men to the store to get the shovel.

I don't think Wullie got a very good education in Glasgow. When the man returned from the store to tell Wullie that there were no shovels in the store Wullie said to him 'I know, but there is no need to be rude about it. If he has no shovels he does not need to return the chit with "there is no f in shovel" written on it.'

What Wullie did not understand was that the Storeman was pointing out that 'shovel' is not spelt 'shufle'.

ALY TOOT

Aly Toot was Aly Mackintosh, sadly another great character who is now gone. Aly was a fabricator and had worked when he was younger on the Forth Road Bridge and had survived a fall of one hundred feet into the Firth of Forth. This is the story I was told of how Aly got the name of Aly Toot.

Aly had started working at the fabrication yard of Mcdermotts at Ardersier in the early 1970s when the building of the Yard was still in progress. Aly was working on the pile rack on the yard; this is an area where lengths of pipe were welded together. Aly stopped and spoke to a sparky who was working on the over-head crane which was being installed on the pile rack. The crane was mounted on rails and it could move along the pile rack to where it was required.

The sparky told Aly that this was a special crane and to make it move you had to shout at it and it would move on the rails. Aly did not believe the sparky so he gave Aly a demonstration. He told Aly all you needed to do was to shout *Toot* at the crane and it would move along the rails. The sparky shouted *Toot* and the crane began to move. What Aly did not know was that another sparky was out of sight and had the control buttons for the crane and was listening to his mate as the pair set Aly up.

So the sparky who was speaking to Aly asked him to try and operate the crane by shouting at it. This Aly did and was amazed as the crane moved along the rails when he shouted *Toot*. Aly called his mates to witness this amazing crane and as he shouted *Toot* the sparky who was out of sight would press the buttons for the crane and Aly would think he was operating the crane.

I do not know how long it took before Aly found out he was' had' but I do know that when we both worked at the Nigg Construction Yard some eighteen years later I would hear someone asking after Aly Toot or as he became known, Toot.

I do not write this as an insult to Aly as he was a very competent and respected worker and as I mentioned at the start of this story was one of the great characters who is sadly missed.

WHO STOLE THE BACON

In Mcdermotts Construction Yard there was an area called the Jacket where large steel structures were constructed. There was shift working and the night shift had just started. Someone had taken a pound of bacon to work to be fried up at the break but omeone had stolen the bacon and the security guard was called from the front gate of the yard to the Jacket to try and solve the crime. Normally security guards are not very enthusiastic when asked to investigate a crime as their wages are very small and they have to work long hours. But as every store or warehouse has its jobs-worth, Mcdermotts security had its over-enthusiastic security guard. I think he was known as Hitler. He was the one who was asked to investigate the crime.

He arrived at the scene of the crime and entered the Supervisor's hut. The Supervisor had just put his men to work and was checking his manpower sheet to see that all his squad were present. The security guard told the Supervisor that he had been asked to try and find out who had stolen the bacon and asked the Supervisor (who I believe was called the Wicker. I will not try and explain why he was called the Wicker as I am sure you will work this out for yourself) if he had seen any suspicious characters at the start of the shift to which the Wicker replied that he had. The security guard asked if he could have their names. The Wicker looked down at his manpower sheet and rhymed off the names of his squad as the security guard noted them down. He continued to note them until he noticed that this was a very long list of suspicious characters and stopped and decided that this might be an opportunity to make a quick exit. I do not think this crime was ever solved.

THE BERMUDA TRIANGLE

This was a term used by the travelling workers who had managed to get lost in Nairn at the weekend after too much alcohol. This was a notorious area in Nairn and a person could disappear between the three main Hotels on the High street.

On Monday morning two workers discussing what had happened to them at the weekend would say, 'It was the Ray Milan'. There was an old movie in which the main character was Ray Milan and in the film he lost his memory so in Parliamo Glesga slang this meant that the person had no recollection of the weekend.

Other slang sayings were:

'Hey, it's a bit Hill Billy tonight '(Chilly) to which the other person would reply, 'Aye, ah know. Ye wouldn't pit milk bottles oot on a night like this'.

Going for A Pony and Trap [toilet]

Going for A Single Fish [the toilet again]

The Tin Pail [The Jail]

A Ruby Murray [Curry]

The S--- Kicking. This may have been an American form of slang and was used to describe a mid-week visit to a Country and Western night out at the Ice-rink in Inverness

DAVY MIDDLE

Davy was working as a trainee welder in one of the fabrication shops at Ardersier in the early 1970's. Davy was welding in the fabrication shop when one of the American Gold Hats (a high heid yin) came round the corner on his tour of inspection, checking on the progress of whatever contract they were working on and stopped to speak to Davy. "Hey Davy, what did you do before you came here?" To which Davy replied, "I had breakfast". I can imagine this American visitor to our shores walking away thinking 'Did this conversation really take place, I asked this young man a question about his previous work experience and he thought I was talking about the meal he had before work'.

THE SHIP-YARD

A man worked at a ship-yard on Clydebank and as he was not working on the Saturday he asked his boy, who was about eight years old, if he would like to be shown round a ship-yard. His son agreed and so they set of to have a look around the ship-yard. They entered the gates of the Yard and the boy said to his father, "Dad, what are those cranes on top of those concrete blocks for?"
His father said, "I'm not sure son, I'll try to find out". They continued round the Yard an his son asked him, "Dad, what is the meaning of the white line that is painted around the side of the ship?" [Plimsoll Line] His father replied, "I'm not too sure about that son".

As they continued around the yard the boy asked about the huge piles of chains lying on the ground beside the ship. His father replied, "I'm don't know what those chains are for son, I must try to find out". As they completed their tour of the Yard the father said to his son, "I hope you enjoyed your tour around a ship-yard son". His son said that he had enjoyed it but he hoped that his father did not mind him asking so many questions. His father replied, "Of course I don't mind you asking questions son. If you don't ask questions, how are you supposed to learn?"

BEN AND THE LETTER

A letter was a disciplinary letter and was issued by managers to employees for things such as bad time-keeping. Of course not all employees took this form of discipline as seriously as the managers and Ben was one of those employees. Ben came from the village of Ardersier and would often take a day off during the week. Ben was working as a pipe fitter at the warehouse on Mcdermotts Yard.

He was working down a hole where pipes were being joined together. Ben was completing the job by wrapping the pipe at the welded joint with Denso-tape. This is a cloth tape covered with grease and would be wrapped round the pipe to protect it from frost or corrosion. As Ben was finishing wrapping the pipe two Gold Hats (Managers) arrived to deliver the letter. One manager was to be a witness and the letter was handed to Ben and he was told why he was receiving a disciplinary letter.

Ben did not seem to take the matter as seriously as the managers as when he took the letter he did not open it but slapped it onto the pipe he was working on and carefully wrapped the letter into the Denso-tape joint he was making and continued to wrap the tape until the letter disappeared.

Ben took his redundancy money from Mcdermotts early on as contracts dried up. He bought a small shop in the village of Ardersier and I am told he took great delight at about two o'clock in the afternoon tapping on the window inside his shop and waving to former workers heading off to start a night shift at the yard.

Of course, the disciplinary letter is now a time capsule and the site used by the oil companies is now zoned for a town and marina at Ardersier. It amazes me how our world and environment changes even in the last 30 years.

GLASGOW HUMOUR

As I have said before I think the Glasgow people have a great sense of humour and I think we Scots do not find it difficult to laugh at ourselves. Here are some examples of Glasgow humour.

A BONE FOR THE DUG

A women goes into a Butchers Shop in Glasgow with her son and asks the butcher for a pound of pork sausages, a half pound of mince, and a bone for the Dug to which her son pipes up 'Hey Ma, when are we getting a Dug?'

THE GHILLIES

This story took place in the early 1980s. My friend Joe Catt and myself had arranged to fish on the famous River Spey for one day. It must have been early in the year, about April, when we headed off from Inverness to Fochabers for our day on this famous river as we would not be able to afford to fish at peak times.

I did not have a lot of fancy fishing equipment at this time as my children were young and we were not well off. I did not have a pair of waders so I wore an old pair of trainers which I used when I played squash. I wore a blue thermal jacket and an old pair of jeans. Joe was more presentable and had a green wax jacket and green waders.

Joe supplied the transport which was an old Fiat two door car. It was green but because of a problem with rust the driver's door was orange. He got this from a scrap-yard. The car had seen better days and Joe had some difficulty in getting good radio reception on the car's radio. This may have been due to the fact that his original car aerial had been ripped off and Joe had replaced it with an upturned metal coat hanger for a car ariel.

We arrived about 9am and drove into the car park of the hotel in Fochabers.
We waited in the middle of the car park for the ghillie who would show us the beat on the river. As we waited a brand new green Range-Rover drove into the car park and stopped beside us. The top of the Range-Rover was bristling with all sorts of rods and landing nets. This was obviously a Toff and this was confirmed when he tried to speak with some marbles in his mouth. He said to Joe and myself, 'I say are you the ghillies' to which Joe replied as if he had rehearsed it, 'No we're not the ghillies. The ghillies are in the bar drawing lots to see who's going to get us'. The Toff looked a bit surprised and headed for the bar to see if he could find his ghillie which he did and headed for the river.

About five minutes later a rather dejected figure appeared from the bar and came across to Joe and myself. We talked to the ghillie and asked about our beat on the river.
The ghillie explained where it was and asked us to drive him to the river. Joe's car had only two doors and the ghillie clambered into the back seat of the car. He did look right smart in his green tweed suit. When he had settled in the back of the car he was about to light up a cigarette when Joe advised him against it as there was a strong smell of petrol fumes in the back of the car probably due to a fuel leak.The ghillie did not light up his cigarette.

We arrived at the river in about ten minutes and we got our rods out of the back of the car and got ready to fish. The ghillie stood beside his boat to see if we wanted to fish out of it. I declined and waded into the river in my trainers and jeans and started to fish. The ghillie looked rather dejected but soon cheered up when Joe gave him a swig out of his half bottle of whisky. Eventually the ghillie decided that his services were not required and as a tip seemed very unlikely he wandered off down the river and headed home. Of course the ghillie knew that there was little chance of us catching a fish as it was early in the season and the water level was low. Joe and I fished the river until the afternoon and eventually gave up after practicing our casting on the famous river.

Some twenty years later I met Joe when he was working in Raigmore Hospital in Inverness. I did not recognize him when he spoke to me as he had shaved off his beard. I reminisced with Joe and talked about the time we had spent a day fishing on the river Spey. I said to Joe that I must have been off my head to have spent hours wading in the cold water in a pair of jeans and trainers and that I did not think I could do this now. Joe said that he thought that I would although I was now in my fifties. Joe also commented on my dress code for our day on the Spey and said he was a bit ashamed of me. I said that he may have been ashamed of me but I was not the one who owned the green Fiat car with an orange driver's door and an upturned metal coat hanger.

Whenever I pass through Fochabers and see the Toffs Hotel on the left hand side I cannot suppress a chuckle as I think about my friend Joe and myself when we had a day out on one of Scotland's most famous rivers.

THE FLY FISHING COMPETITION

Myself and Joe were taking part in a fishing competition on a loch outside Elgin in the 1980s. There were four boats on the loch. Joe and myself were in one boat and six other anglers were in the other three boats. The loch was stocked with rainbow trout and there was a special prize of an automatic fly reel for the person who caught the heaviest fish on the day.

The fishing started at ten o'clock in the morning and I started to cast line as Joe rowed the boat out onto the loch. No sooner had I started to fish when I hooked one and started to play it. I asked Joe to get the landing net ready as it felt like a good fish. This he did and soon he had a fish of about two and a half pounds safely on board. Joe and I now settled down to fish and within a short time I had caught another fish about a pound in weight which Joe netted.

For the next half-hour Joe caught nothing and was muttering something about how he should have just come along as my ghillie as all he seemed to do was net fish for me. I continued to catch trout of about a pound in weight and soon I had filled half a carrier bag. Joe had still caught nothing and asked me about the fly I was using and if I had another fly of the same pattern that he could use. I explained to Joe that we were on a fishing competition and that if I gave him one of my flies he could win the competition with one of my flies.

Towards the middle of the afternoon I relented to Joe's requests for one of the killer flies and Joe put it onto his cast. This did not make Joe's fishing any more successful and he continued to catch nothing along with the anglers on the other boats.

About twenty minutes from the end of the competition Joe took off the fly I had given him and searched his fly box for another fly to try. He pulled out a fly that looked like a bumble bee. In desperation he tied this fly onto the leader and cast the fly and let it sink to the bottom of the loch. About five minutes before the end of the competition Joe wound in his line and was as surprised as I was to see his rod bend: at last Joe had caught a fish. I netted Joe's fish and went ashore with the other boats to weigh the fish to find that the only fish caught on this day came from our boat. So I won the competition and the prize of the fly reel.

For those who are interested in fishing flies I will give the dressing of the fly that did so much damage on the day. The fly is similar to a modern day Viva or a Black Chenille tied on a long shank size ten hook. The only difference is that the throat hackle is a piece of red wool. Eyes can be painted onto the head when the fly is finished and it does not seem to matter if the head is on the ugly side as this seems to add to the attraction of the fly. I fish it on a slow sinking fly line and a fast retrieve makes the marabou wing life like. I have had success with this fly when fishing for brown trout but it seems to be most effective when used to fish for rainbow trout.

HOLIDAY ACCOMMODATION

In the mid nineteen-seventies early in the trout season for the Highlands, probably about April, my friend Woody and myself headed on a Friday night for the West Coast of Scotland into Gods Own Country. We headed for Achiltibuie to try and find some lochs to fish for brown trout. We arrived late on Friday night and Woody was determined to sample a few drinks at the local hotel.

As the night wore on and it started to get dark and other distractions caught my friend's eye, my thoughts turned to our accommodation for the night which was a two-man tent I had brought along. Eventually I convinced him that it was time we looked for a pitch for the tent; reluctantly he agreed with me but by the time we left the hotel it was pitch dark. We went to the local camping park which was on the beach and I attempted to put up the tent.

The wind had got up and the tent pegs would not hold in the sand and we tried to hold the guy ropes down using stones from the beach. All was going well until I realised that the middle pole for the top of the tent was missing. After some searching in the car it was agreed that the pole had been left at home. With very little ceremony I removed the tent from the beach and deposited in the boot of the car. We got into the car and headed back along the road out of Achiltibuie.

On the outskirts of the town we stopped at a disused quarry and in it stood a corrugated shed with no door which was used to store blasting nets. We decided that this would do for the night and we clambered on top of these nets and spent a very uncomfortable night in our new holiday accommodation. It was a very cold night as the wind was blowing from the east and we did not get much sleep. At about six o'clock the next day we could stand the cold no more and decided that we would head home. A disastrous fishing expedition. Before we left, Woody took a photo of me as I clambered out of this tiny shed as a record of one of the most uncomfortable examples of Fishing Lodges or Holiday Homes that we had used in the Highlands.

Some months later Woody was working at the Nigg Oil Yard on the night shift. The conversation turned to holiday accommodation in the Highlands. An English colleague of Woody's was interested to hear him talk about his Holiday Accommodation at Achiltibuie on the West Coast and asked if it would be possible to stay at Woody's Holiday accommodation. Woody told his colleague that it would be no problem and that he could have it free of charge, reminding him that it was very basic and had no toilet facilities.
Woody's friend insisted that he could not accept this kind offer free of charge and it was decided that Woody would accept a bottle of whisky as payment and Woody promised to take a photo of the holiday accommodation into work the following evening.

The next night the photo was taken into work. That is the photo of me clambering out of a tiny corrugated shed at Achiltibuie. Woody said he had to make a quick exit after showing his colleague the photo as he was not very amused to find that he was being made a fool of.
I don't think Woody did get the promised bottle of Whisky.

*Woody fishing on the Fionn Loch above Inverkirkaig with the beautiful mountain
of Suilven in the background*

CHARACTERS

Every town and village will have its great characters, but I believe that the old
characters who are sadly disappearing cannot be replaced. This is because of the
times and life-styles of these people. Today a child will grow up in front of a
computer and will probably work in an office or factory environment, far
removed from past generations whose life was lived mostly outside.

DAN FRIDGE

Sadly Dan has recently departed this world; he was well known and well liked in
Invernes, a giant among characters, a likeable rogue. My stories or yarns about
Dan are all second hand. I would have liked to have had an interview with Dan
but alas it did not happen. Here are some Dan Fridge yarns.

THE GUIDE DOG

Dan and his friend Mapplebeck were rather thirsty one Sunday morning so they headed for the Coach House Inn, now The Snow-Goose Inn, at Stoneyfield on the Nairn Road. The Coach House opened earlier than other pubs on a Sunday morning. When Dan and his friend entered the Inn the manager would not let them in as they were accompanied by a Lurcher dog. The story goes that Dan and his mate went away and returned. This time Dan was wearing dark glasses and had a white stick. When they went into the bar the barman told them that they couldn't come in, as dogs weren't allowed. Dan's friend told the barman that this was Dan's Guide Dog and it had to go everywhere with Dan. When the barman pointed out that the Guide Dog was a Lurcher Dan's friend replied 'Yes I know that but how's he to know that. He's blind.' I believe the outcome of the story was that Dan and his friend got their pints.

A Lurcher dog is a cross between many dogs. Its main characteristics are its long legs. It was built for speed and used in hare coursing. The Lurcher would be released in a field and would chase the hare until it was exhausted and would then dispatch it. As you will gather the dog was far removed from a Guide Dog.

KISHORN

Dan and his friend Mapplebeck were employed as General Operatives or Toilet Cleaners at the Oil Platform Construction Yard at Kishorn on the West Coast of Scotland. The Yard lies below the amazing road which leads from Kishorn to Applecross. This road rises nearly vertically from sea level to the top of the mountains and on to Applecross. I have travelled this road and find it an exhilarating and a hauntingly beautiful place. The scenery is spectacular and I have often thought how difficult it must have been in olden times for those who had to traverse it in winter. With a horse or a pony and trap this journey must have been very dangerous. The road is well worth a visit in the summer time but is not recommended to inexperienced drivers.

My uncle Johnny Goodbrand told me that he worked for British Telecom
laying cables in the 1950's. He said that at that time there were no crash barriers at the side of the road and that a lorry carrying concrete up this road lost control and ended up falling down the mountainside. The driver was killed instantly. Around the 1970's the wrecks of vehicles that did not make it up this road could be seen rusting at the bottom of the mountain.

To get back to Dan and his pal. They were in charge of cleaning the toilets at the Fabrication Yard. The yard employed thousands of men to build concrete structures for The North Sea Oil Industry, and so the number of toilets required was vast. Dan and his mate would get fed up of constantly cleaning so many.

They watched as their clean toilet cubicles would soon have the floors swimming in mud from the workers as they dragged it into the toilets.

Dan had an Idea. They would clean several toilets and close the doors and put old pairs of welly boots under the doors to make it look like the cubicle was engaged. When a worker came in he would think that these toilets with the welly boots showing were Engaged and would wait for someone to come out of one of the toilets that were in use. So Dan and his friend had only a fraction of the toilets to clean. You've got to hand it to these guys - this is clever thinking.

THE DUMP

When I was unemployed in the 1980s I found that there was still part of the old Inverness refuse dump in the Longman where I could dig for old bottles and containers dating back to the late 19th century. As I could not find work I would spend two or three days a week digging at this dump. It was fascinating digging up pieces of history from a bygone age, anything from a clay pipe to various stoneware containers including pots used by dairies such as the Stranraer dairy and the Buttercup dairy. I have about 25 different cream pots and they make an interesting display in my kitchen. These pots were transported north by train and discarded when empty.

I also dug up old Ginger Beer bottles used by local soft drink companies such as Mackintosh, Hossacks, Forest and the Highland Brewery to name a few. I would dig up cups and plates used by the Highland Railway Company. I sold these to a collector as at that time I needed the money. Other items which I dug up include toothpaste containers made out of stoneware and hot water bottles, stone flagons and poison bottles. The poison bottles came in different colours such as cobalt blue, green and amber; these bottles were ribbed down the side so that a person could identify the bottles in the dark by feel.
The enthusiasts who dig old dumps throughout the British Isles use terms which sound as if they come from mining or gold digging. You dig a trench sometimes five or six feet deep throwing the spoil as it was called over your shoulder. The vertical part in front of you was known as the face. If you came across a face with a layer of bottles sticking out this was called a seam. Of course digging could be dangerous and if the face of the trench collapsed on top of you would try and dig yourself out or another digger would help you by digging you out.

A shovel or spade was used to dig the trench and a garden fork was used to carefully prize the bottles and pots from the face. This was done by working from the bottom to the top of the trench. When this was done the trench had filled in and you would have to start throwing the spoil over your shoulder again until you had a new face to search. When I started digging I could only dig down to about three feet but as I got used to it I could dig down to five and six feet. You would continue digging in this fashion until you were worn out and headed home with your bag of treasures to clean and polish.

The thrill of it was that you did not know what you could dig up and of course you wanted to dig up the older and rarer bottles which could be quite valuable. There were old patented glass bottles which would have contained soft drinks. There was the Codd bottle which had a marble trapped in the neck which pushed against a rubber ring using the gas from the drink to seal it. There was also the Hamilton bottle which had a tapered bottom; this patent was designed to seal the bottle by storing it on its side so the cork would not dry out.

THE KNIFE

My friend Woody told me that when he was out of work a friend would call round and ask Woody if he wanted to go to the dump with him. As Woody had nothing better to do he agreed to go along. As they were about to leave Woody's friend asked him if he had a knife. Woody did not understand and asked why he needed a knife to which came the reply, "you will need the Knife for the chairs". This was of course to rip the linings and the material from chairs and couches to retrieve the loose change which had fallen to the bottom of the lining of these pieces of furniture.